EMPOWERMENT OF RURAL WOMEN THROUGH SELF HELP GROUPS

EMPOWERMENT OF RURAL WOMEN THROUGH SELF HELP GROUPS

By

Dr. B. SUGUNA

Associate Professor
Dept. of Women Studies
Sri Padmavathi Mahila Visvavidyalayam
Tirupati (A.P.)

DISCOVERY PUBLISHING HOUSE
NEW DELHI-110002

ISBN: 978-81-8356-096-2

Empowerment of Rural Women Through Self Help Groups

Published by:
DISCOVERY PUBLISHING HOUSE PVT. LTD.
4383/4B, Ansari Road, Darya Ganj
New Delhi-110 002 (India)
Phone: +91-11-23279245, 43596064-65
Fax: +91-11-23253475
E-mail: discoverypublishinghouse@gmail.com
sales@discoverypublishinggroup.com
web: www.discoverypublishinggroup.com

Printed at:
Infinity Imaging Systems
Delhi

PREFACE

The state of Andhra Pradesh has been the focus of attention on the world map primarily due its pro-active government and significant strides made by its Self Help Groups. SHGs are playing an important role in optimization of natural and human resources through people's participation and achieving the goals of Vision 2020. The government of Andhra Pradesh has taken up Women's Empowerment as one of the main strategies to tackle socio-economic poverty. SHG movement through savings has been taken up as mass movement by women, a path chosen by them to shape their destiny for the better. Development agenda of the state in the last few years of placing the people especially women in the forefront has enabled the formation of large number of Self Help Groups throughout the state where women are saving one rupee per day. The state government is making efforts to assist SHGs by providing revolving fund under various programmes.

In this context *Dr. Suguna's* book on *Women Empowerment and Self Help Groups* is very much relevant to the present day situation. The book is an indepth case study of Self Help Groups functioning in Chittoor district of Andhra Pradesh. The major findings, strategies for the sustainability of Self Help Groups and suggestions to strengthen the Self Help Groups of the study are relevant for the effective implementation of the programme. The author has explained elaborately the methodology used and the data analysis is lucid. The book will be highly useful to the students and research scholars of social sciences especially Women's Studies, Social Work, Sociology, Economics and also to the students specializing in Human Development, NGO's and other functionaries dealing with women. I wish the author would bring about many more studies relevant to present day issues of women.

(Prof. Veena Noble Dass)
Vice–Chancellor
Sri Padmavathi Mahila Visvavidyalayam
Tirupati–517 502 (A.P.)

ACKNOWLEDGEMENTS

In carrying out the present project work and bringing it to a successful completion, I have received generous help from a number of people. I place on record here my indebtedness to all of them.

I express my sincere thanks to the University Grants Commission, New Delhi for giving me this opportunity by providing financial assistance in carrying out this project.

I deem it my duty as well as pleasure to express my sincere thanks to the authorities of Sri Padmavathi Mahila Visvavidyalayam, Tirupati for permitting me to conduct this study providing me with all the required facilities throughout the project work.

My sincere thanks are due to Prof. R. Jayasree, Head, Department of Women's Studies for her valuable suggestions in carrying out this work. I also express my deep sense of thanks to all my colleagues in the Department of Women's Studies for their encouragement and co-operation in this endeavour.

My special thanks are due to the Commissioner of Women Welfare and Child Development, Hyderabad also the Project Directors of DRDA in Chittoor, Cuddapah, Kurnool and Ranga Reddy for providing the necessary and valuable information.

I am grateful to the library staff of Sri Padmavathi Mahila Visvavidyalayam for having helped me by providing necessary material in execution of the project work.

I express my sincere thanks to all the sample respondents, without whose valuable co-operation this endeavour could not have been completed.

My thanks are due to Ms. K. Vanisri and Ms. V. N. Lakshmi Soujanya, Project Fellows for their co-operation and assistance in collection of necessary information.

I am thankful to Prof. Kodandarami Reddy, Department of Econometrics, S.V. University, Tirupati for his valuable help in the interpretation of data formulation and adoption of the relevant statistical methods.

Last but not the least I express my sincere thanks to Sri Ramesh, Student Xerox, Tirupati for typing out the whole project report meticulously.

Dr. B. Suguna

CONTENTS

1

INTRODUCTION

Meaning and Concept of Empowerment

The concept of women's empowerment is the outcome of several important critiques and debates generated by the women's movement throughout the world, particularly by the third world feminists. Its source can be traced from the interaction between feminism and the concept of "Popular Education" developed in Latin America in the 1970's (Walters; 1991). The concept of women's empowerment has its roots throughout the world in women's movement.

According to Chandra Shanti Kohli (1997) empowerment in its simplest form means "the manifestation of redistribution of power that challenges patriarchal ideology and the male dominance."

"Becoming Powerful" the liberal meaning of the term "empowerment" is being used today in all spheres of life as a process to strengthen the elements of society. It is both a process and the result of the process. It is transformation of the structures or institutions that reinforces and perpetuates gender discrimination. It is a process that enables women to gain access to and control of material as well as information resources. Gender disparity manifests itself in various forms, the most obvious being the trend of declining female ratio in population.

The 'empowerment' approach was first clearly articulated in 1985 by Development Alternatives with Women for a

New Era (DAWN). This term received prominence in early nineties in Western Countries. In India the Central Government in its welfare programmes shifted the concept of development to empowerment only in the Ninth Plan (1997–2002) and observed the year 2001 as 'Women Empowerment Year'.

Definitions

According to Adams (1996), "Empowerment is the means by which individuals, groups and communities to take control of their circumstances and achieve their own goals, thereby being able to work towards helping themselves and others to maximize the quality of their lives. Dubhushi (1997) considered empowerment as exercising control over ones lives, firstly on resources of financial, physical and human and secondly on beliefs, values and attitudes.

The Social Work Dictionary (Barker, 1991), defines empowerment as "the process of helping a group or community to achieve political influence or relevant legal authority".

According to Zippy (1995), empowerment represents "a means for accomplishing community development tasks and can be conceptualized as involving two key elements giving community members the authority to make decisions and choices and facilitating the development of the knowledge and resources necessary to exercise these choices".

According to Pillai. J.K. (1995), "Empowerment is an active, multidimensional process which enables women to realize their full identity and powers in all spheres of life. Power is not commodity to be transacted; nor can it be given away as aims. "Power has to be acquired and once acquired, it needs to be and once acquired, it needs to be exercised, sustained and preserved."

According to Bandura (1986), "Empowerment is the process through which individuals gain efficacy, defined as the degree to which an individual perceives that he or she controls his or her environment."

While discussing empowerment Jo Rowlands (1997) has identified four different forms of powers.

- — Power over—control or influence over others which is an instrumentation of domination;
- — Power to—generative or productive power which creates new possibilities and actions without domination;
- — Power with—a sense of the whole being greater than the sum of the individuals, especially when a group tackles problems together ;
- — Power from within—the spiritual strength and uniqueness that resides in each one of us and makes us truly human. Its basis is self-acceptance and self-respect which extend, in turn, respect for and acceptance of others as equals.

Though the interpretation 'Power to' and 'Power with' empowerment is concerned with the process by which people become aware of their interests and how those relates to the interests of others but also participates in decision making and influence such decisions.

It is difficult to measure empowerment. There is no single method for measuring it. It should be understood and defined through indicators. Indicators of empowerment should encompass personal, social, economic and political change. Empowerment is a term generally used to describe a process by which powerless people, conscious of their own situation, and organise collectively to gain greater access to public service or to the benefits of economic growth.

Empowerment is also the process of challenging existing power relations and of gaining greater control over the sources of power. The goals of women's empowerment are to challenge patriarchal ideology to transform the structures and institutions that reinforce and perpetuate gender discrimination and social inequality and to enable poor women to gain access to and control of both material and informational resources. It can change existing power relations by addressing itself to the three dimensions of material, human and intellectual resources. Empowerment cannot occur as a revolution but only as evolution.

Components

The components of empowerment are as follows :

— Women's and men's sense of internal strength and confidence to face life

— The right to make choices

— The power to control their own lives within and outside the home, and

— The ability to influence the direction of social change towards the creation of a more just social and economic order nationally and internationally.

Stromquist (1995), in her article on educational empowerment for women, interprets empowerment as a "socio-political concept that goes beyond formal political participation and consciousness raising. She argues that a full definition of empowerment must include cognitive, psychological, political and economic components". She explains that :

◆ The cognitive component refers to women having an understanding of the conditions and causes of their subordination at micro and macro levels. It involves making choices that may go against cultural expectations and norms.

◆ The economic component requires that women have access to and control over productive resources, thus ensuring some degree of financial autonomy. However, she notes that changes in the economic balance of power do not necessarily alter traditional gender roles or norms.

◆ The political entails that women have the capability to analyse, organise and mobilise for social change, and

- The psychological component includes the belief that women can act at personal and social levels to improve their individual realities and the society in which they live.

Stromquist notes that there is general agreement that these components are interrelated.

Empowerment as a process of a community or a group there of gaining autonomy and control over one's life. As a result of the empowerment, the empowered should become agents of their own development, exercising choices, selecting their own agenda and changing their status in the society. In the context of gender and development, empowerment should be viewed more as a process than as an end product. It is a dynamic process changing according to circumstances. It applies to the individual as well as the collective. At the individual level, empowerment involves building up the self–image and self-confidence as well as the critical faculties to think, decide and act. On a collective plan, empowerment means enabling women collectively to take control of their own lives, to set their own agenda, to organise each other and make demands on the state and the society for change.

Process

Empowerment as an individual and collective process is based on the following five principles :

- self-reliance
- self-awareness
- collective mobilization and organisations
- capacity building
- external exposure and interaction

Empowerment is a long process. It has to pass through different stages. In the first stage, women should be trained to look into the situation from a different perspective and recognize the power relations that perpetuate their oppression. At this stage, the women share their feelings and experiences with each other and build a common vision and mission. In the second stage, the women tried to change the situation by bringing about a change in the gender and social relations. In the third stage, the process of empowerment makes them more mature to realise the importance of collective action.

As empowerment seeks to alter the gender and power relations, there could be a certain social or gender conflicts. The process of empowerment could also face certain obstacles emanating from the patriarchal system, traditional beliefs and political system. The results of empowerment, however, will not be confined to women. The other member of the families will also benefit from the empowerment process.

Measures

Empowerment is a planned and its nature and quality of relationship over time can be assessed. Changes in power relations were a definite part of the empowerment process. There was a tendency to progress from dependency through independence towards increased interdependence. It is not difficult to measure empowerment ; but the difficulty lies in achieving it.

The Gender Empowerment Measure (GEM) used variables constructed explicitly to measure the relative empowerment of women and men in political and economic spheres of activities namely participation, decision making and power over resources. Any meaningful attempt to measure empowerment would have to go beyond measuring the transfer of resources (physical, financial, human) to the least powerful.

Journey Towards Empowerment

Dis empowerment	Empowerment
Exploited	Affirmed
Insecure	Confident
Controlled	Competent
Victimized	Assertive

Dependence .....Independence.......Interdependence
---------------------------------->---------------------------------

If empowerment was to be measured in changed relationships, change would need to be detected in both sides of the relationship. Those who were involved in the process of empowerment were the right persons to measure their empowerment.

Significance

The term 'empowerment' has gained significance and prominence recently among policy makers and researchers. in the field of women's studies and social work it is viewed with a holistic perspective and it can be classified as social, educational, economical, political and psychological empowerment. To quote Thomas and Pierson, empowerment referred to user participation in services and to the self help movement generally, in which groups took action on their own behalf, either in cooperation with or independently of the statutory services. Empowerment is concerned with how people may gain collective control over their lives, so as to achieve their interests as a group and a method by which social workers seek to enhance the power of people who lack it.

Strategies

Empowerment can be activated through five strategies. Education to promote the level of awareness, knowledge, information and skills of a woman is an important part of the strategy. Awareness is a pre-requisite for challenging the forces of oppression status que. It results in greater participation of women in decision making with in and outside the family. The economic approach to empowerment seeks to alter the economic status of women by attacking the forces which cause gender division of labour, gender gap in wages, lack of control for women over their material resources etc. The economic approach emphasizes development of women's skills, promotion of their savings and investment and enlarged economic opportunities. The third approach namely, development approach attributes poverty to their powerlessness and the lack of adequate access to health care, education and services resources. Yet another approach believes that women's empowerment requires awareness of a complex factors causing disempowerment of women. This approach advocates collective organisation of women as well as gender sensitisation, gender planning and strategy and consciousness raising activities. More recently, an organisational approach has been advocated which believes that organised women can alter the gender and social relations in favour of women both in public and private lives. Finally, political approaches to empowerment believes that women can be developed on par with men, if politics are purged of violence, electoral malpractices, unscrupulous struggles, etc. and were made value based. This would, however, require greater participation of women in active politics.

Empowerment could take place at two levels, individual and collective. Individual empowerment is a process of personal empowerment involving self-esteem, dignity, self-respect and self-perception. But the problems affecting the collectivity of women require collective empowerment. Restructuring power relations, changing social values and norms require intervention at the collective level. Collective empowerment aims at transforming collective conciseness, values an attitudes. The problem of securing better access to education skills and employment, material resources and political power can be tackled only at the collective level. This requires effective organisation among women, mutual help and certain amount of sacrifice.

Self-reliance requires acquisition of physical and mental strength through solidarity, sharing and caring for each other. Self-awareness, on the other hand implies knowledge of living conditions and the factors promoting those conditions. Collectivization and organisation, therefore are called for to change the living conditions through collective effort, pooling and sharing of resources, time and experience. But the poor women need to acquire capacity to work in groups and to play different roles. They must have constant interface with the outside world—the government officials, the politicians, civil society institutions and other groups of poor. The groups must acquire the skills of interaction with external environment.

Indicators of Women's Empowerment

The Draft Country Paper–India for the Fourth World Conference on Women held at Beijing in 1995 proposed the following qualitative and quantitative indicators for evaluating women's empowerment :

(*a*) *Qualitative Indicators*

- Self-confidence understands what she wants, expresses it and tries to get it, feels proud of herself has positive self-image
- Articulation
- Awareness about health, nutrition, legal rights, political activities, government policies and programmes
- Less burden of work and more leisure time
- Changing role and responsibilities within the family
- Decrease in violence within the family
- Changing attitudes towards tradition and customs like child marriage and dowry
- Physical mobility—walk freely with in the village, go to city or town, to banks, post office, go for shopping, cinema, exhibition and visit relatives
- Become member of women's group or any other people's organisation
- Self-identity—identifies herself positively
- Decision making power within the family regarding number of children

- Education of children, marriage of children, budgeting of the family, income and purchase or sale of family property
- Changed attitudes towards women's participation in politics and willingness to participate in the politics
- Control over individual and family income
- Access to resources like land, house, jewellery, house site, etc.
- Access to information, knowledge and skills.

(b) *Quantitative Indicators*

- Increase in age at marriage
- Reduction in fertility rate or number of children
- Becoming beneficiaries of development programmes
- Visible changes in physical status/nutritional status
- Improvement in literacy level ; and
- Becoming member of a political party or local self-government.

Empowerment of Women in India

Indian Constitution in its fundamental rights has provisions for equality, social justice and protection of women. These goals are yet to be realised. Still women continue to be discriminated, exploited and exposed to inequalities at various levels. So the concept of empowerment as a goal of development projects and programmes has been gaining wider acceptance.

By empowerment women would be able to develop self-esteem, confidence, realise their potential and enhance their collective bargaining power. Women's empowerment can be viewed as a continuum of several interrelated and mutually reinforcing components (Marilee, Karl, 1995). They are :

- Awareness building about women's situation, discrimination and rights and opportunities as a step towards gender equality. Collective awareness building provides a sense of group identity and the power of working as a group.
- Capacity building and skill development, especially the ability to plan, make decisions, organise, manage and carry out activities to deal with people and institutions in the world around them.
- Participation and greater control and decision making power in the home, community and society.
- Action to bring about greater equality between men and women.

Thus empowerment is a process of awareness and capacity building leading to greater participation, greater decision making power and control and transformative action. The empowerment of women covers both an individual and collective transformation. It strengthens their innate ability through acquiring knowledge, power and experience.

Constitutional guarantees, legislative measures and policies advocating women's concern and presented in the various Ministries, documents namely Women and Child Development, Science and Technology, Ministries namely Health and Family Welfare, Labour, Rural Areas and Employment, Urban Affairs and Employment, Agriculture and Welfare had listed out their programmes and achievements.

The Ninth Plan (1997–2002) had made its commitment to the objective of "empowering women as the agents of social change and development". The twelve salient strategies spelt out focused on empowering women by making women economically independent and self-reliant. It was being hoped that the strategies would be realized through the National Policy for empowerment of women.

Remarkably Self Help Groups were considered to be one of the strategies to mark the beginning of major process of empowering women.

Committee on the empowerment of women was constituted on April 1997 to improve the status of women. It consisted of 30 members, 20 members of Lok Sabha, 10 members of Rajya Sabha of Indian parliament. The committee presented its first report on "Developmental Schemes for Rural Women" to Lok Sabha on 21 April 1999. The functions of the committee included examining the measures to secure women's equality, status and dignity in all matters and considering the reports of National Commission for Women. They also undertook on-the-spot visits in connection with the representatives of elected Panchayat Raj institutions and Municipal bodies.

Planning Commission (1999–2000) had given specific emphasis on empowerment of women, besides the continuation of the important initiative programmes like Rural Women's Development and Empowerment Project (RWDEP) was introduced in the states of Uttar Pradesh, Madhya Pradesh, Bihar, Haryana, Karnataka and Gujarat for a period of five years. The overall objective of the project is to enable empowerment of women by establishing Self Help Groups which will improve the quality of their lives through greater access to and control over resources.

In order to alter the scenario the year 2001 has been declared as the Year of Women Empowerment and in order to help women focused on issues of importance, each month had a theme as follows :

Women Empowerment Year, 2001

Month	Theme
January	Human rights for women
February	Economic empowerment of women
March	Social empowerment of women

(Contd.)

April	Women in difficult circumstances
May	Women and technology
June	Women and governance
July	Women and education
August	Women and health
September	Nutrition
October	Women and media
November	Entreprenuership in women
December	Vision for the future

Emergence of Self Help Groups : A New Women's Movement For Social Change and Women's Development

All over the world there is a realization that the best way to tackle poverty and enable the community to improve its quality of life is through social mobilization of poor, especially women into Self Help Groups. Ever since Independence a number of innovative schemes have been launched for the upliftment of women in our country. Indian government has taken lot of initiatives to strengthen the institutional rural credit system and development programmes. However formal sector credit agencies find it difficult to reach vast majority of rural people. The problem highlighted above required a complete paradigm shift where the flexible and responsive system meets the needs of the rural poor. Viewing it in the welfare programmes of ninth five year plan (1997–2002) and shifting the concept of "development to empowerment" the Indian Government adopted the approach of 'Self Help Groups (SHGs)' to uplift the rural poor women focusing on the following aspects :

They are :

— Direct involvement of women in programming and management

— Effective collaboration with community organization
— Organising and strengthening of women's Self Help Groups (SHGs)
— Sensitisation and advocacy of gender just society
— Organising women in different groups to undertake certain productive activities to earn their livelihood and to develop rural community.

Empowerment of Women Through Self Help Groups

The empowerment of women through Self Help Groups (SHGs) would lead to benefits not only to the individual woman and women groups but also for the families and community as a whole through collective action for development. These groups have a common perception of need and impulse towards collective action. Empowering women not just for meeting their economic needs but also through more holistic social development.

Origin of Self Help Group Movement

The concept of SHG serves the Principle "by the women, of the women and for the women". The origin of SHG is from the brain child of GRAMIN BANK of Bangladesh, which was found by the economist, Prof. Mohammed Yunus of Chittagong University in the Year 1975. This was exclusively established for the poor.

Self Help Group is a small economically homogeneous and affinity group of rural poor which is voluntarily ready to contribute to a common fund to be lent to its members as per group decision, which works for group's solidarity, self-group, awareness, social and economic empowerment in the way of democratic functioning. The Self Help Group movement became a silent revolution within a short span in the rural credit delivery system in many parts of the world. It has been documented that nearly 53 developing countries including India, have taken up this on a large scale. In 1997, World Micro Credit Summit at Washington converged the developed and the developing countries to tackle the serious problem of poverty by using micro credit as a tool to empower the poorest sections. A global movement has been launched to reach 100 million of the world's poorest families by the year 2005.

Meaning of Self Help

Self help is one of the most fascinating yet frustrating aspects of development. It is a dynamic process that transcends the narrow boundaries of any given aspects of development. The purported benefits from selfhelp are multifarious. Self-help is a fundamental tenent of recent expounded strategies of basic needs and self-reliance.

Self help is both a means and a goal within the strategy of basic needs. It is a means with which to achieve goals of minimum requirements of private consumption *i.e.,* adequate food, shelter and clothing and community services *i.e.,* safe drinking water, sanitation, public transport, health and education. It is also identified as a tool, people should participate in making the decisions which effect them. As SHGs were initiated to combat the weakness in private credit formal financial institutions have been able to mobilize savings from the persons or groups who were normally expected to have savings and also recycle the same effectively.

SHGs pool resources amongst the members and thus meet the credit needs of the poor. SHGs have emerged from the felt needs of the people and they have evolved their own methods of working. SHGs helps in creating a platform for sharing of experiences collective knowledge, building problem, solving and resource mobile satisfaction and other institutions. In SHGs the autonomy of the women groups is never undermined and all decision making is entirely in their hands. This group helps women to build confidence in themselves as decision markers, planners and to work collectively in a democratic manner.

Tremendous amount goes into these groups, it may be worth notion of that most developmental groups tend to spend 4–10 hours a month in the early stages. The SHG activity is thus a win-win situation, wherein the poor women get access to credit as well as make profit.

Persons/Institutions Help in the Formation of SHGs

DADA, Non Governmental Organisations (NGO's) Social Workers, Health Workers, Village Level Workers, Banks, Bank Personnel, Farmers Clubs under the Vikas Volunteer Vahini (VVV) programme of NABARD play a very important role in the formation of SHGs.

Concept of Self Help Group

'All for all' is the principle behind the concept of Self Help Groups (SHGs). It is mainly concerned with the poor and it is for the people, by the people and of the people. SHGs, a mini voluntary agency for self-help at the micro level has been a focus on the weaker sections particularly women for their social defence. SHGs has got great potential in creating awareness on day-to-day affairs, promoting in savings habit, developing self and community assets, increasing the income level, increasing the social power etc. The concept of SHGs generates confidence, self-scrutiny and self-reliance.

Self Help Groups (SHGs) formed in rural India usually consisted of fifteen to twenty members hailing from a certain locality with similar socio-economic backgrounds. The unregistered groups operated on the principles of mutual trust, co-operation and interdependence. Preference in memberships was offered to the poorest of the poor, handicapped, widowed, deserted and dalits. The leaders were selected from members of the group. Where there was nobody to help the helpless mass the concept of "Self Help" could be introduced. Hence, it would be enable them to comprehend the need and to design the remedial measure accordingly. One of the significant features of "Self Help" is, to make people not to relay on the government or non-governmental organisations to improve the infrastructure facilities needed the village. Hoping to achieve this target SHG women are making collective efforts.

Objectives of Self Help Groups (SHGs)

The following are the main objectives of Self Help Groups :

— To inculcate the habit of saving and banking habit among the rural women.

— To build up trust and confidence between the rural women and the bankers.

— To develop group activity so that various welfare and developmental programmes can be implemented in a better way with the participation of these women groups.

— To achieve women and child welfare programme goals by actively involving these women groups in Universal Immunization Programme, small family norm, Universal Elementary Education etc.

Characteristics of SHGs

The following are the chief characteristic features of SHGs :

- Small size.
- Identical interest/social heritage/common occupation, homogeneity, affinity.
- Intimate knowledge of members of intrinsic strength, needs and problems.
- Flexible and responsive.
- Democratic in operations.
- Simple documentation.
- Collective leadership, mutual discussions.
- Group solidarity, Self Help, awareness , social and economic empowerment.

Benefits

The benefits of SHGs are as follows :

— A via-media for development of savings habit among the poor.

— An access to large quantum of resources.

— A window for better technology/skill upgradation.

— Availability of emergent, consumption/production credit at the door step.

— Access to various promotional assistance and

— Assurance of freedom, quality, self-reliance and empowerment.

Functions of SHGs

In view of carrying out the empowerment of women, the SHGs are expected to take on certain functions which are essential documentation on the happenings of the SHGs and their involvement with the wider society is considered to be vital. Small savings details are maintained by the members themselves.

Best Practices in Self Help Groups

Group Formation Methods

Getting a group formed takes time and skills. Development workers must pay frequent visits to the community where the group is to be formed and devote time to talk to the people and getting to know them. Some sort of investigation into the problems of people and their response patterns, beforehand will surely help. There is no one best way to form groups, however, the following sequence of events have been found to be consistent in yielding good results :

- A meeting with local opinion leaders and elders to develop mutual confidence.
- Use of rural mass media like burrakatha, street plays, puppet shows, folk songs, etc. for sensitising and motivating community members.
- Providing clear picture about the theme of Self Help Group programme soon after the cultural event.

- Enlisting support of community volunteers for animation purposes and to do the talking with people.
- Holding of focus meetings of interested members to clarify doubts and address fears.

Membership in Self Help Group

It is important that people from poor households are made aware and made to recognize the significance of collective efforts in solving problems that seem impossible with individual efforts, by voluntarily deciding to put their efforts together to help increase their access to financial services, economic services like technology, training in skill and enterprise management, material support and marketing facilities, etc. besides a host of other social services.

Homogeneity Factor

The greater the extent to which individuals share activities, the more they will interact and the higher the probability that they will form a group. Interaction enables people to discover common interests, likes and dislikes, attitudes or sentiments. There are other important factors which encourage homogeneous group formation *viz.,*

- ***Gender :*** Gender focus of groups has been quite successful in promoting gender concerns, particularly in the context of economic empowerment of women.
- ***Neighbourhood :*** People who live in the same neighbourhood are likely to form stronger groups than people who live in different areas.
- ***Community :*** People with similar social background exhibit similar coping behaviour in times of crises hence will be able to extend mutual support.
- ***Occupation :*** People in similar occupation tend to be cohesive and group action is often found successful in confronting common problems.

Besides these, other factors like age, physical or social disability, management of community resource/asset are also being tried out for building up community organisations.

Membership Requirements

- Size of group is normally restricted to 15–20 members to facilitate participatory processes.
- Members of a group should be at least 18 years of age.
- Members should be aware of rights and obligations of membership.
- Members must share understanding on objectives and vision of group.
- Finally, membership by mutual selection is a solitary means to build group solidarity.

Mutual selection process entails the participant to expressly indicate the list of all people who could be trusted with their money. Persons with negative characteristics tend to be left out of such formed trust groups and those with the positive attributes tend to be included.

Rights and Obligations of Members

- Every member has a right to determine goals, objectives and vision of the group.
- Every member has a right to participate in every activity of the group.
- Every member has a right to participate in group meetings and decision making.
- Every member has a right to participate in the leadership function.
- Every member has right to access loans from the pooled corpus funds of the group.
- Every member has a right to share in the group's wealth.
- Every member has a right to scrutinise group's records and inspect property.

- Every member has a right to withdraw from membership in genuine circumstances.
- Every member is under obligation to accept goals, objectives and vision of the group.
- Every member is under obligation to participate in all group activities.
- Every member is under obligation to make oneself aware and abide by group norms and rules.
- Every member is under obligation to participate in group meetings and decision making.
- Every member is under obligation to contribute minimum agreed thrift amount to the group.
- Every member is under obligation to act with diligence in discharge of group responsibilities.
- Every member is under obligation to discharge debt liability contracted by the group.
- Every member is under obligation to participate in supervision of group finances/businesses.
- Every member is under obligation to defend the group at all fora.

It is quite interesting to note that the rights and obligations of members are almost convergent mainly on account of Self Help Group being a member owned, managed and controlled institution. Every ordinary member is also a part of management. Hence, transparency is the watch word.

Governance in Self Help Groups

Strong savings and credit groups owned and managed by the community itself need competent and committed development facilitators, strong cadre of leaders, and enlightened and alert members. Hence the governance of Self Help Groups that promotes democratic traditions is crucial for its success. Evolution of norms or rules and regulations for self-governance, participatory decision making, diligence and self-discipline among group members coupled with strong enforcement mechanism are sufficient conditions for transparency in group operations. These rules and regulations are not mere statements but reflect the understanding of group norms by members through their conduct in group activities. Rules and regulations of the group, therefore, need to apprehend conflict situation in day to day functioning of group and provide ready solutions. These could broadly cover :

- Groups to have unique name to give it a distinct identity
- Goals and objectives of group formation
- Membership issues—optimal size, entry norms, exit policy
- Extraordinary issues concerning membership—expulsion and co-option of members
- Leadership structure—positions, roles and responsibilities
- Positioning of leaders—tenure, selection and change process
- Financial services—savings and credit products
- Fund management—cash management, interest rates, expenditures
- Decision making—decision making apparatus, styles and record keeping
- Enforcement of decisions made by the group
- Enforcement of group norms—discipline procedure
- Relationships management with service agencies—Banks, SHPI/DRDA, etc.

While stability of group membership is strongly encouraged, it is possible that a few members could be co-opted into the groups to attain optimality in group size, alternately delinquent members could be expelled, in which case the groups could undertake a situational analysis and take appropriate decision. However, core objectives of the group and rule for self-governance should not be lost sight of.

Leadership Responsibilities

It is apt to realise that leadership in a Self Help Group is a Verb and not a Noun. The range of leadership responsibilities include the following :

- Providing guidance for group activities
- Assisting in information sharing among group members
- Helping define problems and identify solutions
- Facilitating appraisal of group performance
- Encouraging members to offer ideas and opinions
- Resolving conflicts and disputes between group members
- Conducting meetings and facilitating group decisions
- Organising, implementing and coordinating group plans
- Facilitating financial transactions during group meetings
- Maintaining and keeping records of accounts
- Maintaining a bank account on behalf of the group
- Representing the group's interests to outside bodies
- Conducting negotiations and doing business with other organisations
- Rendering truthful and correct accounts to members

Considering the wide ranging responsibilities of leaders in Self Help Groups, responsibility sharing mechanism by assigning different leadership roles to several members must be worked out. This entails :

- Grouping of leadership responsibilities and identifying leader positions
- Affording clarity in roles and responsibilities of different leadership positions
- Selecting leaders for discharging expected leadership roles on consensual basis
- Developing systems and procedures where ordinary members are required to assist leaders in discharge of routine functions
- Providing in built mechanism for rotation of leadership at least once in two years with clear succession plans for smooth change-over of leadership, similar to that found in rotary clubs
- Adopting a methodology for changing leaders in case of non-fulfillment of expected roles

Meetings

Group meetings include times when members gather either periodically or at short notice to discuss the activities of the group and decide on its future actions. All activities in Self Help Group revolve around meetings at which members access savings and credit services, share experiences, learn from each other and also receive education and training.

- Meeting is a forum for group action and facilitates information sharing among members
- Meetings are to be convened at regular intervals as per the convenience of the members
- While frequency of meetings is guided by the convenience of members, the critical determinant is the ability of members to discharge financial obligation to the group. In other words, thrift, credit and record keeping functions must converge with the meeting at least once a month

- Meetings must be held at a mutually decided place, date and time. In other words, meetings are conducted at same place, on the same day and at same time each time they are held
- In the absence of common meeting place, meetings could be held at the house of each member by rotation
- Active participation in the deliberations by all members must be encouraged with expression of free and frank views. However, involvement of non-members in the decision making process should be strictly objected to
- Structured agenda for group meeting with definite sequence of activities to be pursued (*viz.*, attendance, review of decisions of previous meeting, thrift, repayments, loans and social issues) will make meetings effective
- Deliberations on other social and community issues together with routing financial matters are found to consolidate group dynamics
- Sharing of various responsibilities among the members during the meeting process
- Attendance of members taken before commencement of deliberations at the meeting enables effective member participation
- Meetings should have near–full attendance of members, any absence of members must be viewed seriously
- Penal provisions like fines, penalties, etc. must be enforced for late coming/leave without prior intimation
- Chronic absenteeism in meetings are generally discouraged by withholding or delaying other pecuniary benefits to members

Savings Function

Poor look for saving services from formal financial institutions. Without a safe place to put their savings, the poor tend to invest it in "assets" such as gold, silver, livestock, etc. which can be pawned or sold in times of need. Thrift contributions by members to the group must be perceived as a savings product serving long term financial security needs. As such savings are generated by poor households either by refraining from consumption or postponement of their not so urgent needs. The thrift contributions reflect confidence of members on the group and is seen as an index of their stake in the process. Thrift management is, perhaps, the most important function in a Self Help Group. Some of the best practices in this include :

- Thrift collection could commence from first meeting itself
- Periodicity and quantum of thrift decided by group members themselves keeping in view the ability of poorest member among them to pay the agreed amount at predetermined intervals
- Minimum compulsory thrift contributions to be made by all members
- Withdrawals against compulsory thrift contributions are not permitted unless the member withdraws from primary membership
- Groups must insist for on-time contribution by members
- Groups must collect thrift contribution in the presence of all members during the meetings only
- Thrift collections must be utilised for lending to group members and must not be kept idle
- Penal provisions like fines, penalties, etc. must be enforced against late payment or default in thrift
- Chronic default in on-time thrift contributions by members are generally discouraged by withholding

or delaying other pecuniary benefits to members. At times penalties for late/non-payment include fees, denial of higher loan amounts or longer waiting periods for loans

- Delayed thrift contributions must not be received outside meetings
- Additional or seasonal savings are encouraged by a few number of groups. But it is again desirable to have equal savings without interest implications keeping in view the weak fund management capability of many groups. However, whenever optional savings are offered it is suggested that suitable compensation (interest) is provided to address the equity question among various members
- It is desirable to make payment of thrift amount to a member withdrawing from the group for genuine reasons
- Continuity of thrift is the Jugular of Self Help Group process and any attempt to obstruct or discontinue it after receipt of Revolving Fund, Subsidy, Grant or even a Bank Loan can only be a self-inflicting move

Credit Function

Providing credit access to members of poor household on sustainable basis is the primary objective of Self Help Group. A well conceived loan programme in a Self Help Group will enhance its attractiveness to the members. These loans are often given for various purposes without insistence on collateral but are available at cost. There is no compulsion to avail of loan facility, as such those who avail loans have to make a choice to pay the cost, or have no credit at all. Some of the best practices in the area of credit function management include :

- Self Help Groups typically offer small, short-term loans for meeting emergent and consumption requirements only to their members
- The internal lending must preferably commence from the data of first pooling of savings. Need based lending is strongly recommended by active groups
- Loans are extended keeping in view the nature of need of particular member. Preference in borrower evaluation is, however, given to those who are regular in attendance at meetings and timely payment of thrift amounts
- Group must have a system of giving differential priorities to several purposes for taking loaning decisions. Here urgency of purpose is given precedence while selecting a borrowing member
- Groups must establish a process to assess of credit requirement for arriving at loan quantum, efficacy of such system need to be seen in the context of particular Self Help Group
- In a few groups, the loan quantum is in proportion to the individual member's total thrift contribution. Decision of groups indicating differential loan quanta based on the purpose and person availing the loan reflects their maturity
- All credit decisions must be taken at the meetings only after giving due consideration to opinion of all members
- Large loans to members are suitably collateralized considering the risk perception of the group. Often, groups go in for chattel financing wherein a borrower offers a critical productive asset as security for loan
- Terms of credit like interest rate and schedule of loan repayments are negotiated and conveyed clearly to the borrowing member

- Flexible repayment schedules are worked out by groups taking into consideration the various income-flows of the household and repayment capacity of the member concerned
- Monthly or even weekly repayments (wherever weekly meetings are held) of both principal and interest payments are found to be convenient to both borrowers and the group to liquidate the loan liability
- Separate schedules for principal and interest payments may be stipulated as they are easy to comprehend even by illiterate borrowers
- Loans could be issued to the borrowing members in the presence of other members of the group
- Groups ensure proper end-use on credit as also management of asset, wherever created. This practice must be continued at frequent intervals till the loan is fully repaid by the borrowing member
- Concurrent loans are generally discouraged by most groups in view of small fund base. But wherever they are given, rigorous appraisal must be undertaken on the purpose, genuine need of borrower and her performance in the earlier loan.
- Reward for on-time repayment may be given to members in the form of future access to higher loan amounts
- Penal provisions like fines, penalties, etc. must be enforced against late payment or default in loan repayment
- Chronic default in on-time loan repayment by members are generally discouraged by withholding or delaying other pecuniary benefits to members. At times penalties for late/non-payment include fees, denial of higher loan amounts or longer waiting periods for further loans.

- Continuity of need based internal lending will strengthen Self Help Group processes and any attempt to obstruct or discontinue it after receipt of Revolving Fund, Subsidy, Grand or even a Bank Loan can only be a self-destructive move.

Fund Management in Self Help Groups

Mobilising micro thrifts is only part of a comprehensive savings service Self Help Groups. Small savings from resource-poor households need operative protection against loss of deposits. Misappropriation in savings and credit groups as well as imprudent lending from internally generated deposits threaten the security of savings programme. They have to be shielded against the financial and non-financial risks. It is, therefore, considered necessary that high standards are set in the area of fund management which cover the following :

- Group fund generally comprises member thrift, interest earned on internal loans, fines and penalties levied on defaulting members, loans and grants received in the name of the group. The groups are not expected to discriminate between the sources of fund for meeting loaning requirements. In other words, the savings, loan repayments, interest payments, fines and penalties paid by members will be pooled in the meeting for on-lending to the group members.
- Efficient cash management in a meeting reflects the fund management capability of the group. Idle funds are a drag on the group.
- Responsibility sharing in cash management at each meeting on rotation basis for assisting the group leaders will not only promote transparency but also enhance fund management competence among group members.
- Managing of savings account with local branch is another important area in fund management. All

cash collections made at a meeting may be deposited into the bank and withdrawals made for disbursing the loans. While members could take turns for depositing the cash into bank, the persons authorised and the borrower concerned could draw the money from bank. However, groups maintaining up to date records could consider extending loans out of pooled fund during the meetings itself. Periodic reconciliation of accounts with bank transactions is considered useful.

- Preparation of micro-credit plans in groups by groups improves considerably the credit absorption capacity as it entails acquisition of planning and financial skill among group leaders.
- In the initial stage only short term loans are extended, usually for periods ranging from 3–12 months, to enable larger number of members access credit facility from the group. However, insistence on monthly repayments from borrowing members will accelerate the velocity of lending within the group, which also partially reflect equity in loan access to group members.
- Groups must have a policy on interest rates. Most groups charge interest rates that are linked to contemporary market rates. It is also desirable to build in risk factor in the interest rate structure in long term.
- Generally interest is not paid to the members on the compulsory savings. Even in cases where interest is computed on compulsory thrift contributions the same is merged with the member savings rendering the very process infructuous.
- Coming to interest rate on loans, a few groups have been charging differential interest rates to their borrowers keeping in view the purpose of loan which can be considered good. However, the groups

are not expected to soften their rates in the short term with the receipt of grant or loan funds from institutional sources. It must be appreciated that the interest charged on loan is a source for raising additional capital to fund the corpus base. However, the interest maybe charged on outstanding loan amounts as against interest rates charged by a few on EMI or flat rate basis.

- Members must be made aware of their cumulative thrift contributions and loan outstanding.
- Investment of pooled savings in a common asset (even a productive one) and blocking internal lending will in fact run counter to the objective of giving sustainable credit access to poor households. Further, the risk of investing entire corpus in a singular activity is fraught with risks.
- Groups incurring regular expenditure towards cost of bank transactions, honorarium to book keeper etc. could consider collecting additional amounts every month from their members to avoid erosion of loaning funds.
- A few groups have been holding small cash balance, say of Rs. 200/- to Rs. 300/- to give hand loans to members for meeting emergent credit requirements.

Record Keeping

Record keeping is possibly the most crucial function in a Self Help Group often confined to the periphery. An efficient record keeping assumes significance for promoting transparency in the system considering the need for providing safety of micro deposits pooled in savings and credit programmes. An effective information system that supports their self-management efforts is sine-quo-non for sustainability of Self Help Groups. Such system can be considered effective when it is easily understood and appeals to cognitive abilities of ignorant and illiterate community.

Besides, it must be credible, verifiable and facilitate quick recall of stored information in the perception of users. Some of the best practices in record keeping area could reflect upon the following issues :

- Critical self-awareness must be created among groups on issues relating to record keeping
- Groups must assume the responsibility for safe keeping of records
- Group members must be trained to recognise books of accounts and their structure
- Groups must be encouraged to discuss on nature and contents of records
- Groups must be encouraged to hire services of local book keeper to upkeep records in case of non-availability of literate members in the group capable of writing the records
- Groups must be strongly encouraged to compensate for services rendered by book keeper
- Groups must ensure that books are updated while the meeting is in progress
- Groups must ensure that book writer reads out the nothings made by him in various books
- Groups must develop a practice of closing the books of accounts by year end
- Cross checking of books across groups (peer audit) could be encouraged for audit purposes
- Groups must encourage its members to learn to read and write their own books in the long run
- Members must cultivate habit of confirming entries in member passbook

Group Vigilance

The corpus fund of a group is entirely contributed by its members and hence they alone must ensure that the fund is managed and controlled by them without any outside interference whatsoever. There is no alternative to alertness of members and their participation in group meetings. Some of the best practices discussed earlier also go in strengthening the group vigilance and control mechanism. These include :

- Responsibility sharing mechanism where members assist leader in conduct of meeting
- Practice of leadership rotation coupled with clearly laid out succession plan
- Preventing outsiders from handling cash, even for training purposes
- Responsibility fixing for handling cash during meeting and holding imprest cash thereafter
- Practice of tallying cash inflows and outflows at the end of each meeting
- Practice of clarifying memberwise cumulative savings and loans position every month
- Responsibility to deposit cash and withdrawal from savings bank account on rotation basis
- Practice of bank reconciliation on periodic basis
- Ensuring end-use of credit by helping the borrowing member in purchase of assets, if any
- Regular review of deviant behaviour of members in attendance, thrift or loan repayment
- Enforcement of group discipline through fines and penalties system in a transparent manner
- Practice of rotating members accompanying leader for training and review sessions

Banking Relationship

Self Help Groups are primarily savings and credit groups and availing savings and credit services from local banks is a logical extension of their growth strategy to meet increasing credit demand from members. Moreover, accessing savings services from banks will provide safety to the pooled funds. It is expected that groups will demonstrate desired maturity in terms of group and financial dynamics leading to inculcation of banking habits in the groups. It would also make possible the bringing about of general improvement in the nature and scale of operations that would accelerate economic development.

- Open savings account in group's name with the service area branch concerned
- Regular operations in the group's savings account will help build healthy relationship with bank
- Groups to assess their future fund requirements and articulate the credit gap in micro-credit plans
- Groups to have clarity on issues relating to eligibility conditions, credit entitlement and legal obligations arising out of credit linkage with banks
- Groups and banker must hold discussions at loan appraisal stage for enabling banker to arrive at a credit decision
- Terms and conditions of credit extended by banks including implication of joint and several liability in the event of credit linkage must be clearly understood by all members of the group
- Groups must assimilate bank loans with their corpus fund by extending need based loans to those members who could not access loans earlier from out of pooled savings. Here, the group must take care not to deviate from the financing norms (quantum of loan, rate of interest, repayment period) already laid down for giving loans out of their pooled thrift amounts merely because outside funds are injected into the group corpus
- Groups must ensure on-time payment of bank loans by setting aside a portion of total collections made in each meeting for honouring repayment

obligation to the bank. In other words, groups will square up the default amount of any borrowing member and pass on the instalment amount to the bank as per contracted repayment schedule

- Continuity of thrift and need based internal lending even after receipt of bank loan will strengthen Self Help Group processes and any attempt to obstruct or discontinue it can only be a self-inflicting move.
- Banks must reward for on-time repayment by means of repeat and higher finance.

SHGs also promoted democratic culture and provided women with opportunities to imbibe norms of behaviour that are based on mutual respect. Hence they were able to foster concern even in internal lending of loans based on the individual needs and priorities. It provided a firm based for dialogue and co-operation in programmes with other institutions like Government departments, co-operatives, financial and Panchayat Raj Institutions.

The SHGs engaged not only in productive economic activities but also in social empowerment and capacity building of rural women. Health education, medical facilities, literacy, alternative agriculture practices, leader- ship qualities and team building are other activities of SHGs. Various studies revealed that SHGs ensured we feeling among the members achieving the group cohesiveness and accorded a social identity to the rural women. It also enabled them for collective bargaining while keeping up their dignity. The "non-productive and non-assest worthy", naive village women had become agents of social change and economic development of the community through decentralized means of empowerment.

Empowerment, therefore, is closely linked to economic independence. Nothing succeeds better than the self help. And when efforts are supported by the Government and private agencies the results could be extremely gratifying.

Today, there are two lakh self-help group women focussed around economic activities like savings, collective marketing, promotion of individual enterprise and in the process of moving into the main stream of society. In the process, leadership qualities blossom, discipline prevails and true democracy beginning to function. This also helps add value to the work they do, their families and their communities.

Stages of SHGs

The following are the 3 stages of evolution of SHGs.

- — Group formation.
- — Capital formation through the revolving fund and skill development.
- — Taking up economic activity for income generation.

Formation of SHGs

Formation of SHGs begins with an assessment of members strength. People are motivated to collect information an initiatives they have taken in the past to resolve problems and to initiate collective or group action. Information on income and borrowings and seasonality on the availability and use of natural resources and skills and markets on people perception of poverty and its causes of the various social groups in society, their mutual interdependence should also be collected.

Participatory Rural Appraisal exercises including meetings with various groups in the villages and outside with poor families in public and private a structural analysis of the society and exercises that brings to the surface gender biases in society within caste, creed, colour and employment benefits are appropriate instruments to collect information that is necessary in order to identify affinity groups. The members are saving money regularly. An account is open in the nearest bank or post office. Basic records such as attendance register, minutes book and savings ledgers are maintained.

Identification of SHGs

It must be understood that the basis of the Self Help affinity group exists prior to any intervention. The members are linked by a common hand like caste, sub caste, blood community, place of origin or activity. The interventions whether formed by the NGO, Bank or Government must have the experience to identify these natural groups which are commonly called affinity groups which links together the group members therefore is not primarily the need for credit but a capital stock of relationship built on mutual trust.

Of group members on a degree of social and economic homogeneity the group offers the best opportunity to realize the latent and often suppressed aspirations to develop economically and socially. The regular visits to the village meetings with informal groups gathered around tea shops, temples, water spots, markets, provision shops, milk collection centres, special care or few of the popular strategies used. Involvement of the entire village in a common action like desalting a pound or building around also helps to identify these groups, provided people organize the action themselves. It is noticed that it is encouraged to plan such projects, people tend to work in affinity groups.

Promotion of SHGs

SHGs are organic in terms of their development and pass through various phases before getting stabilized. To begin with SHGs have to stabilize the regularity of meetings, participation of members, maintaining of books, regular transactions of savings and leading among members with little or no outside support. The process of stabilization is influenced by various factors which include the span of SHG, awareness of members, leadership, interaction among members, training programmes and common activities undertaken by the group.

According to Dhan Foundation (1998) the preformation period of the group may be 1-2 months in which the initial identification of the group is done. During the formation period 3-6 months often self-selected 15-20 women form a SHG. Evolving of rules and norms for conducting the meetings takes place. They begin to save and maintain accounts. SHG members training and animators training programmes are arranged. Literacy and numeracy classes are also conducted for the members.

In the stabilization period 7-12 months SHGs regularize and increase savings. They start and repaying of loans. They begin to interact with other groups, Government and private institutions. Groups are linked to the banks and they begin to avail bank loans. SHGs join the cluster and block level federations in the panchayats. They begin to involve in common issues too. It includes of their living conditions, basic amenities, etc. NGOs are expected to reduce their direct interactions with the SHGs. So that the groups would become self-reliant.

During growth period 19-25 months, the linkage with the banks are intensified. NGOs enable them to venture into productive activities. Their cluster level activities are improved. The expansion and diversification period (25 months and above) focuses on creating assets for individual members or for the groups. Each SHG has to become an individual institution and the federations have to manage to supervise the SHGs. NGOs support in formalizing linkages with other institutions.

Social Movement

A social movement has thus begun wherein rural women started saving money by forming themselves into small groups and come together to decide all issues which affect their lives. During the last 5-6 years saving movement caught up the imagination of women as a means of Self Help Groups through which they are trying to mould their destiny. It may be rated as the most successful anti-poverty programme and contribution to women's empowerment and the expectation continue to be high, the need for taking a look at the present status has been felt. Thus women empowered by economic independence can contribute to society and at the same time improve their standard of living and self-esteem can be demonstrated and taken to logical and where an empowerment of women folk will take their rightful place in the path of progress.

Social movement is therefore, a prolonged action of deprived homogeneous group to strengthen the roots of the group in the society to which the group belongs. The collective mobilisation for action directed towards transformation of the structure of a system can be understood as a social movement. Social movement which is an off-shoot of social change may appear in any one of the stages of change depending upon certain system conditions. Mukerji. P.N. (1997) analyses social movement as a productive of social structure and the consequences for it is an agent of change. Social movement can further be distinguished on the basis of change and ideology of the movement. Movement can be aimed at reforms in social life or oriented in bringing about changes in superordinate or subordinate relationships and finally towards bringing about revolutionary change in every sphere of life and in basic values.

Women's Movement

Throughout the changes of history, women have collectively struggled against direct and indirect barriers to their self-development and their full social, economic and political participation. The women's organisations started struggle for women's rights in the early part of the 20th Century. At present women's movement focuses its attention on equality and influenced policy and planning of the government for development and empowerment.

Women's movements in general are directed by objectives like to promote better understading of the process of social, technological and environmental changes to contribute to the pursuit of human rights and to develop alternative concept, approach and strategies to bring out necessary changes for bettering the life of women with autonomy, freedom and full rights of the citizens.

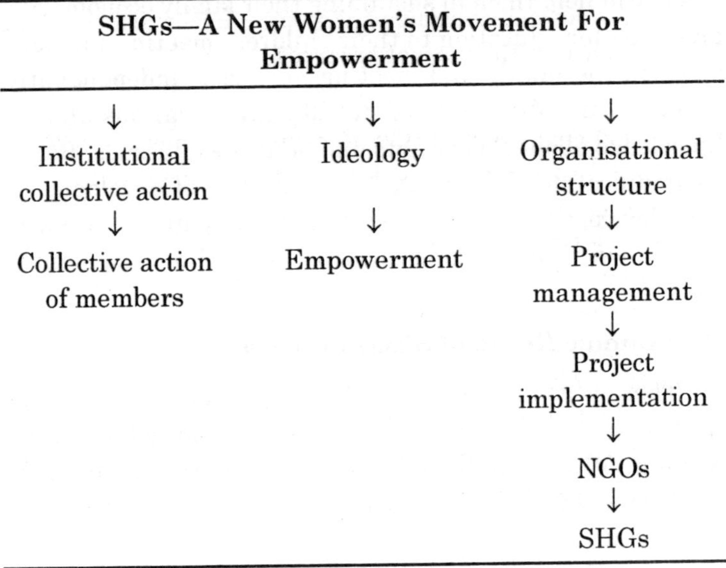

In order to understand the activity of SHGs in the frame work of movement it is found that SHGs are organised to manage their economic activities better and are gaining empowerment in directions which are appropriate to their needs, interests and constraints. The SHGs help to gain confidence from an increase in their relative financial independence and security. The increase in the literacy skills of SHG members is another indicator of social change and development. The animators, representatives and SHG members get training for this work by NGOs in order to develop leadership quantities such as organizing meetings, liasion with NGOs and government officials, coordinating and motivating the members.

Decision making is the ultimate level of development and empowerment of women. It signifies that women have started taking control over their lives and situations through attending group meetings, public functions, involving in income generating activities and joining other women in social causes. The collective and integrated activities of the SHGs will help them in sustaining their family economically giving better education to their children, meeting financial crisis in the family and meeting any crisis independently. The SHG members are sensitised against various abuses, knowledge about their rights and other social issues. Better communication skills is another indicator of development. This develops their ability to interact and communicate with each other, thus bringing about integrated development of women.

Programme Route of SHGs in India

There is a very strong role for civil society organizations in this process. The state cannot, and should not, empower women. What the state can do is to create enabling conditions which legitimize a change in women's position (Srilatha, 1997). In promoting SHG movement both Governmental and non-governmental agencies are involved. SHG movement had been designed to benefit women, especially in rural belt, towards providing them social status and identify. Hence, Central Government had invited the state Governments to involve in the SHG movement. A two-day conference of Rural Development Ministers of different states was held at Hyderabad on 23-24 June, 2001 to launch at least one SHG or self-employment activity in each of the 14 lakh habitation in the country by 2004. In India, Tamil Nadu and Andhra Pradesh had been successful in SHG movement. Therefore the Central Government had asked the State Governments of Orissa, Bihar, Jharkhand, Chhattisgarh, M.P. and U.P. to provide the same momentum for their development. The model given on page 43 was followed in all over India.

Programme Route of SHG's in India

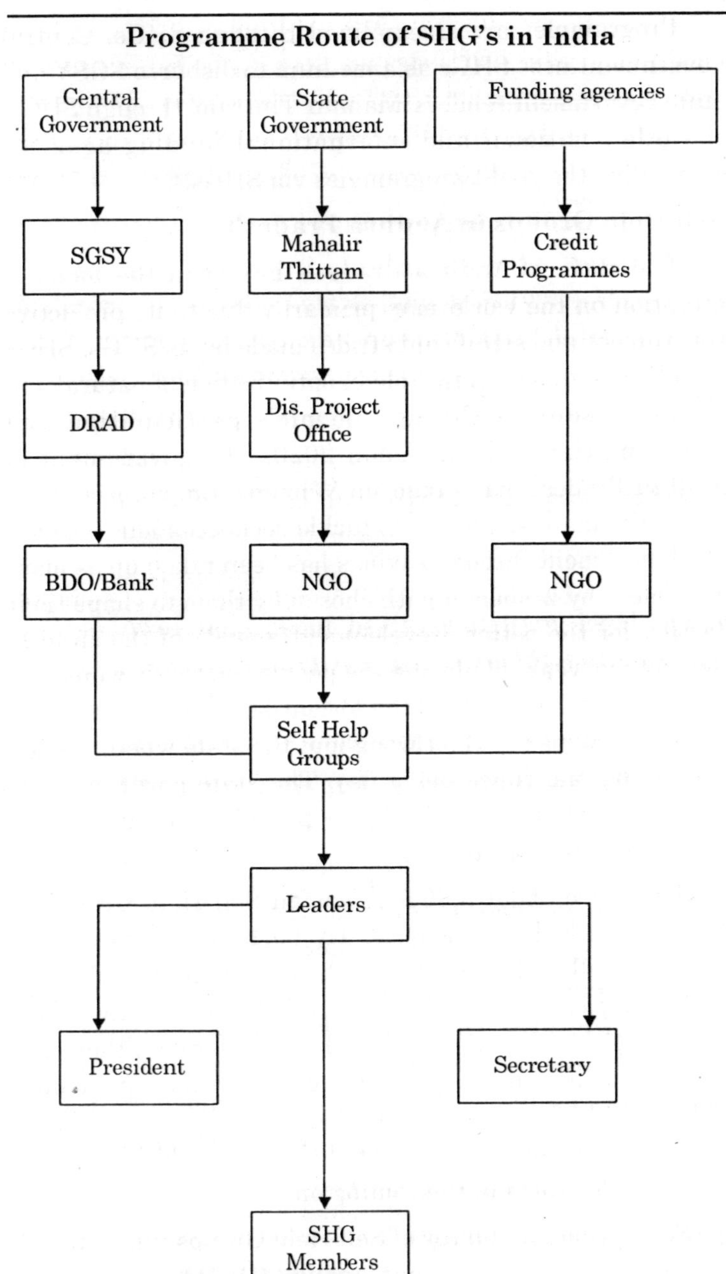

Programmes are streamlined through SHGs. Central government uses SHGs as a medium to disburse SGSY and state government renders 'Mahalir Thirram' through SHGs. the other national and international funding agencies streamline the credit programmes via SHGs.

Self Help Groups in Andhra Pradesh

The state of Andhra Pradesh has been the focus of attention on the world map primarily due to its pro-active government and significant strides made by its SHGs. SHGs are playing an important role in optimization of natural and human resources through people's participation and achieving the goals of Vision 2020. The government of Andhra Pradesh has taken up Women's Empowerment as one of the main strategies to tackle socio-economic poverty. SHG movement through savings has been taken up as mass movement by women, a path chosen by them to shape their destiny for the better. Development agenda of the state in the last few years of placing the people especially women in the forefront has enabled the formation of large number of self help groups (SHGs) throughout the state where women are saving one rupee per a day. The state government is making efforts to assist SHGs by providing revolving fund under various programmes.

There are about 4,36,579 women Self Help Groups in Andhra Pradesh, covering nearly 65,48,685 of rural poor women. Andhra Pradesh alone has about half of the Self Help Groups existing in the country. Up to 1994, only 10,000 groups were functioning and in the last six years there is a massive scaling up in Self Help Group activities. An amount of Rs. 1043.78 crores is mobilized as corpus with these groups so far and it is estimated that it would increase to Rs. 1,500.00 crores in the coming one year.

Socio-economic survey of Self Help Groups conducted by District Rural Development Agency (DRDA) in different districts has indicated that the scheme has helped women earn additional monthly incomes ranging from Rs. 1500/- to Rs. 1800/- depending on the economic activities taken up. In addition, women have taken up initiatives in improving their socio-economic status by participating in governmental programmes such as family planning, pulse polio, AIDS awareness, small family norm, promoting their nutritional and educational status, awareness on environment, public health through sanitation and clean drinking water etc. A large number of women from Self Help Groups participate in Janmabhoomi Programme regularly as active partners for the development of their villages.

It has been planned by the Government to cover all the rural poor women under Self Help Groups in the next 4 to 5 years. It is programmed to cover at least one woman from a BPL (Below Poverty Line) family as a member of Self Help Group in next two years. So far, all the habitations in the state have at least one Self Help Group. The Government released Rs. 44 crores during 2000-01 to assist 44,000 groups covering 6.6 lakhs women @ Rs. 10,000 as revolving fund to each group. This is in addition to Government of India grant of Rs. 4.5 crores. NABARD, Commercial Banks and Regional Rural Banks are providing direct assistance to the Self Help Groups under the "Self Help Linking Scheme" of NABARD.

Due to massive self help movement, there is a perceptible improvement in the socio-economic status of the rural women. Due to constant efforts of the government, women have become very active, assertive and are concerned with the issues relating to them and their surroundings.

Right from the beginning, NGO's in Andhra Pradesh are working for the cause of women and more than 200 committed NGO's have been involved in facilitating the formation of self help groups and efforts for their sustenance.

NGOS are working in close coordination with DRDA's in training and capacity building, skill development training programmes building self help group centered organizations, etc.

It is heartening to note that out of 100 million women in the world, three million out of these are going to be in Andhra Pradesh itself. In fact out of 2.10 lakh DWCRA groups in the country 79,000 are in Andhra Pradesh and the efforts are to cover every eligible self help groups under DWCRA. In addition to these efforts Department of Women and Child Welfare also covered 4,000 groups under income generating activities scheme (IGAS) and spent 14 crore assisting 60,000 women.

Accordingly, the Government of Andhra Pradesh has taken up the theme of women's empowerment as one of the main agenda items to tackle rural poverty and socio-economic issues. Self help movement through thrift and savings has been taken up as a mass movement by women– a path chosen by the women to shape their destiny. Development agenda of the state in the last few years has been to place the poor, especially the women (below poverty line) in the forefront. This has facilitated formation of a large number of self help groups throughout the length and breadth of the state. There are more than 30 lakh women from weaker sections of the society who have become members of these groups and 22 lakh women are saving one rupee a day and rotate the money through a group interaction which starts as a process of empowerment. The State government is consciously making efforts to assist these self help groups by providing revolving fund under DWCRA. The women of Andhra Pradesh have saved more than Rs. 105 crore and the Government has given Rs. 115 crore as working capital grant. The following table shows the status of self help groups in the state of Adhhra Pradesh.

Table—1.1. Status of self-help groups in Andhra Pradesh

	1999-2000	*2002-2003*
Total Groups (Nos.)	3,73,044	4,36,579
Women covered (Members) (in lakhs)	50.65	58.501
Women savings (Rs. in crores)	420.45	783.20
Govt. Assistance (Rs. in crores)	404.54	630.16
Total corpus (Rs. in cores)	824.99	1413.36
Loan mobilised from banks under SHG linkage programme (Rs. in crores)	886.28	931.81
Average Savings per Groups (Rs.)	11258.00	17939.00
Average Credit per Group (Rs.)	23750.55	29261.00
Average Corpus per Group (Rs.)	22088.85	32376.00
SHGs upto year 1994 (Nos.)	10,000	—
SHGs initiated in 1999-2000 (Nos.)	95,000	—
SHGs initiated in 2000-01 (Nos.)	60,000	—

All over the world there is a realiztion that the best way to tackle poverty and enable the community to improve its quality of life is through social mobilization of poor, especially women into self help groups.

The macro policy of the state has attempted to address, through these Self Help Groups, the issues which plague the poor like accessing social services, safe drinking water, shelter, right to information and livelihood. The improvement in the socio-economic status of these women is expected to become the largest organized anti-poverty initiative anywhere in the world.

The following table-2 shows Districtwise cumulative progress of SHGs in Andhra Pradesh.

Table—1.2. District-wise cumulative progress of SHGs in Andhra Pradesh upto 31 March 2002

Sl. No.	*Name of the District*	*Cumulative No. of SHGs Provided with Bank Loan up to 31 March 2002*	*Cumulative Bank loan disbursed up to 31 March 2002*
1.	Adilabad	6,806	145.00
2.	Anantapur	6,984	232.72
3.	Chittoor	11,982	344.60
4.	Cuddapah	2,680	154.65
5.	East Godawari	34,765	805.86
6.	Guntur	7,981	189.55
7.	Karimnagar	14,480	206.02
8.	Khammam	13,141	192.92
9.	Krishna	14,852	237.58
10.	Kurnool	6,399	144.52
11.	Mahaboobnagar	11,653	318.23
12.	Medak	11,832	217.17
13.	Nalgonda	8,032	186.90
14.	Nellore	6,203	205.73
15.	Nizamabad	7,953	144.93
16.	Prakasam	7,077	175.49
17.	Rangareddy	8,152	217.50
18.	Srikakulam	19,722	332.41
19.	Visakhapatnam	12,635	265.43
20.	Vizianagaram	4,459	67.80
21.	Warangal	18,848	211.91
22.	West Godawari	7,078	215.65
	Total	2,43,714	5,212.57

Source : MCID, NABARD (2002) : "NABARAD and Micro Finance", 2001-2002.

The following flow chart shows the functions and support systems for SHGs in Andhra Pradesh

Flow Chart on Functions and Support Systems for SHGs in A.P.

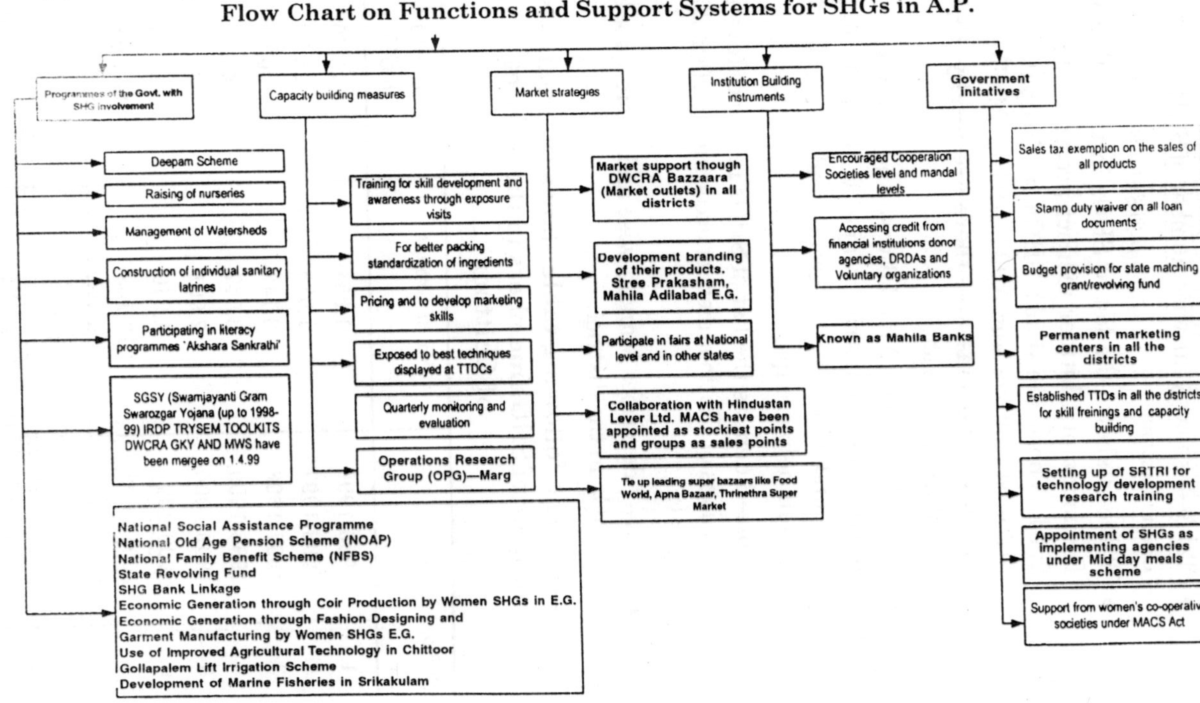

Status of Self Help Groups in the District of Chittoor

- Table–3 shows year-wise number of SGHs/members in the district.
- Table–4 shows the list of SHGs in three Revenue Divisions of Chittoor district according to 2000-2001. There are 3,331 SHGs in Tirupati, 3,893 SHGs in Chittoor and 5,934 SHGs in Madanapalli Revenue Divisions and there are totally 13,158 SHGs in the district.
- Table–5 describes Mandal-wise and Caste-wise list of SHGs in the district. Majority *i.e.,* 6,287 SHGs come under mixed caste groups and there are 2,701 SC self help groups.
- Table–6 depicts the list of SHGs in three Revenue Divisions of Chittoor district according to 2003-2004 records.
- Table–7 describes Mandal-wise and Caste-wise list of SHGs in the district.

Table—1.3. The following table shows the year-wise number of SHGs/members in the district of Chittoor

Sl.No.	*Year*	*No. of Groups*	*No. of Members in SHGs*
1.	1995-1996	1,954	25,402
2.	1996-1997	1,985	25,805
3.	1997-1998	3.142	40,846
4.	1998-1999	3,567	46,371
5.	1999-2000	2,901	37,713
6.	2000-2001	1,940	25,220
7.	2001-2002	13,158	1,71,054
8.	2002-2003	19,330	2,51,290
9.	2003-2004	32,341	4,20,433
	Total	80,318	10,44,134

Table—1.4. List of self help groups in three revenue divisions of Chittoor District-2000-2001

Sl. No.	*Revenue Divisions*	*No. of SHGs*
1.	Tirupati	3,331
2.	Chittoor	3,893
3.	Madanapalli	5,934
	Total	13,158

Table—1.5. Mandal-wise and caste-wise list of self help groups in the district of Chittoor 2000-2001

Sl. No.	*Mandal Name*	*No. of Homogenic Groups*					*Total*
		SC	*ST*	*BC*	*OC*	*Mixed*	
1	*2*	*3*	*4*	*5*	*6*	*7*	*8*
1.	Chittoor	108	1	52	21	85	267
2.	Gudipala	64	0	16	12	66	158
3.	Yadamarri	58	2	40	41	130	271
4.	GD Nellore	77	1	11	27	64	180
5.	Puthalapattu	79	3	51	43	58	234
6.	Penumuru	55	1	38	32	44	170
7.	Bangarupalem	51	0	17	23	121	212
8.	Thavanampalle	71	3	24	17	92	207
9.	Irala	84	3	49	21	65	222
10.	S.R. Puram	35	2	16	6	107	166
11.	Vedurukuppam	57	4	19	50	82	212
12.	Ramachandrapuram	40	6	13	70	46	175
13.	Vadamalapeta	61	10	56	9	79	215
14.	Palasamudram	37	0	20	11	14	82
15.	Putturu	69	12	61	15	145	302

(Contd.)

1	*2*	*3*	*4*	*5*	*6*	*7*	*8*
16.	Karvetinagaram	42	2	25	8	97	174
17.	Narayanavanam	64	6	85	1	17	173
18.	Nagari	63	4	34	10	54	165
19.	Nidra	75	4	37	5	38	159
20.	Vijayapuram	53	3	31	0	62	149
21.	Chandragiri	80	13	29	33	117	272
22.	Pakala	52	1	45	45	126	269
23.	Pulicherla	40	4	38	48	51	181
24.	Tirupati (Urban)	2	0	4	0	21	27
25.	Tirupati (Rural)	65	9	60	17	147	298
26.	Renigunta	94	10	150	12	88	354
27.	Srikalahasti	78	15	45	25	96	259
28.	Yerpedu	87	27	70	18	162	362
29.	Thottambedu	38	8	23	14	111	194
30.	B.N. Kandriga	44	8	42	10	92	196
31.	K.V.B. Puram	28	9	34	2	143	216
32.	Satyavedu	41	1	13	2	61	118
33.	Varadaiahpalem	88	9	34	8	87	226
34.	Nagalapuram	35	7	31	3	113	189
35.	Pichatur	51	5	51	8	55	170
36.	Madanapalli	30	3	60	33	123	249
37.	Nimmanapalli	19	0	19	3	68	109
38.	Kurabalakota	12	1	99	59	84	255
39.	B. Kothakota	18	6	52	40	122	238
40.	Peddamandyam	11	2	27	9	59	108
41.	Thamballapalle	16	10	43	22	101	192
42.	PTM	18	0	13	24	142	197
43.	Molakalacheruvu	25	1	30	13	139	208
44.	Vayalpadu	31	2	27	10	71	141
45.	Gurramkonda	13	0	44	50	60	167
46.	Kalakada	22	1	19	21	46	109

(Contd.)

1	*2*	*3*	*4*	*5*	*6*	*7*	*8*
47.	Kalikiri	23	2	20	8	59	112
48.	Pileru	16	6	37	36	103	198
49.	Yerravaripalem	15	1	34	13	64	127
50.	Rompicherla	4	1	13	41	94	153
51.	Chinnagottigallu	23	3	20	12	123	181
52.	K.V. Palle	31	9	18	18	54	130
53.	Punganuru	24	10	57	31	132	254
54.	Chowdepalle	18	1	41	16	106	182
55.	Ramasamudram	11	0	27	11	79	128
56.	Sodam	19	1	24	7	68	119
57.	Somala	28	2	57	25	58	170
58.	Pedda Panjani	29	3	37	26	198	293
59.	Palamaner	25	6	20	17	77	145
60.	Gangavaram	10	1	16	5	108	140
61.	Baireddypalle	13	0	7	2	41	63
62.	V. Kota	25	6	42	30	195	298
63.	Ramakuppam	40	23	42	20	235	360
64.	Gudupalle	8	0	49	4	119	180
65.	Santhipuram	15	2	71	5	202	295
66.	Kuppam	43	3	149	15	223	433
	Total	2701	299	2578	1293	6287	13158

Table—1. 6. List of self help groups in three revenue divisions of Chittoor District-2003-2004

Sl. No.	*Revenue Divisions*	*No. of SHGs*
1.	Tirupati	8,196
2.	Chittoor	8,745
3.	Madanapalli	15,400
	Total	32,341

Table—1.7. Mandal-wise and caste-wise list of self help groups in the District of Chittoor 2003-2004

Sl. No.	*Mandal Name*	*No. of Homogenic Groups*					*Total*
		SC	*ST*	*BC*	*OC*	*Mixed*	
1	*2*	*3*	*4*	*5*	*6*	*7*	*8*
1.	Chittoor	93	28	133	81	69	404
2.	Gudipala	100	31	144	87	74	436
3.	Yadamarri	128	39	184	111	95	557
4.	GD Nellore	110	34	158	96	81	479
5.	Puthalapattu	108	33	155	94	80	469
6.	Penumuru	93	28	133	80	68	402
7.	Bangarupalem	111	34	160	97	82	484
8.	Thavanampalle	128	39	183	111	94	556
9.	Irala	113	34	162	98	84	492
10.	S.R. Puram	104	32	149	90	77	452
11.	Vedurukuppam	159	48	229	138	118	692
12.	Ramachandrapuram	101	31	146	88	75	441
13.	Vadamalapeta	72	22	104	63	53	314
14.	Palasamudram	52	16	74	45	38	224
15.	Putturu	85	26	122	74	63	371
16.	Karvetinagaram	122	37	175	106	90	532
17.	Narayanavanam	104	32	149	90	77	451
18.	Nagari	5	17	79	48	41	238
19.	Nidra	93	28	134	81	69	406
20.	Vijayapuram	79	24	114	69	59	345
21.	Chandragiri	102	31	147	89	76	445
22.	Pakala	135	41	194	118	100	588
23.	Pulicherla	143	43	205	124	106	621
24.	Tirupati (R)	259	79	371	225	191	1125

(Contd.)

1	*2*	*3*	*4*	*5*	*6*	*7*	*8*
25.	Renigunta	166	51	239	145	123	724
26.	Sri Kalahasti	130	40	187	113	96	567
27.	Yerpedu	186	57	267	162	137	808
28.	Thottambedu	115	35	166	100	85	502
29.	B.N. Kandriga	110	34	158	96	81	479
30.	K.V.B. Puram	157	48	225	137	116	683
31.	Satyavedu	91	28	131	79	67	396
32.	Varadaiahpalem	97	29	138	84	71	420
33.	Nagalapuram	109	33	156	94	80	472
34.	Pichatur	84	26	121	73	62	366
35.	Madanapalli	118	36	170	103	87	515
36.	Nimmanapalli	78	24	112	68	58	341
37.	Kurabalakota	110	34	158	96	81	479
38.	B. Kothakota	102	31	147	89	76	445
39.	Peddamandyam	101	31	145	88	75	440
40.	Thamballapalle	87	27	125	76	64	379
41.	PTM	95	29	136	82	70	411
42.	Molakalacheruvu	100	30	143	87	74	434
43.	Vayalpadu	108	33	156	94	80	471
44.	Gurramkonda	91	28	130	79	67	394
45.	Kalakada	90	27	128	78	66	389
46.	Kalikiri	69	21	99	60	51	301
47.	Pileru	104	32	150	91	77	453
48.	Yerravaripalem	82	25	117	71	61	356
49.	Rompicherla	86	26	123	74	63	372
50.	Chinnagottigallu	77	24	111	67	57	337
51.	K.V. Palle	94	29	135	82	69	408
52.	Punganuru	116	35	166	101	86	504
53.	Chowdepalle	109	33	156	95	80	474
54.	Ramasamudram	87	26	124	75	64	376
55.	Sodam	128	39	184	111	95	557
56.	Somala	125	38	179	108	92	541

(*Contd.*)

1	*2*	*3*	*4*	*5*	*6*	*7*	*8*
57.	Pedda Panjani	161	49	231	140	119	701
58.	Palamaner	67	20	96	58	50	292
59.	Gangavaram	164	50	236	143	121	714
60.	Baireddipalle	149	45	214	130	110	648
61.	V. Kota	201	61	288	175	148	873
62.	Ramakuppam	154	47	220	134	114	668
63.	Gudipalle	116	35	167	101	86	506
64.	Santipuram	160	49	229	139	118	694
65.	Kuppam	213	65	306	185	158	927
	Total	7438	2264	10672	6468	5498	32341

2

REVIEW OF LITERATURE

The present study is designed with a view to examine the impact of Self Help Groups on empowerment of women. A comprehensive review of literature is essential for any good research endeavour as it provides background information to aid researcher in designing and analyzing research work. Since the early 1980s, a large number of studies have examined the various dimensions of micro finance programmes and women empowerment. Several international organizations like Action-Aid, UK, CGAP (Consultative Group to Assist the Poorest) and Overseas Development Authority (ODA) have conducted case studies and organized workshops in various countries. The workshops had looked mainly into the experiences of different countries and the impact of micro finance programmes in a cross-cultural perspective. Other sources of information include published and unpublished materials including materials from the Micro-Credit Summit (February 1997 and 2001) and action research programmes of IRMA, NIRD and CIRDAP Digest. An attempt is made in this chapter to give a brief account of literature related to empowerment of women and Self Help Groups under the following headings.

- — Studies on Empowerment and Need for Self Help Groups
- — Studies on Characteristics of Self Help Groups
- — Studies on Effects of Self Help Groups

Studies on Empowerment of Women and Need for Self Help Groups (SHGs)

From the development experience of many western countries, it was found that there is correlation between women empowerment through education, poverty entitlement and dismantling of gender discrimination in employment and in the holding of public and political offices and those in the professions and particularly in judiciary and economic growth in its totality encompassing capital formation, human resource development, technology advancement and professional managerial competencies. Thus, women have been recognized as being critical to the success of the development process, pointing out that the government's major thrust has been on providing women with access to the factors of production (Beijing Conference, UN Report, 1995).

Batliwala (1994) identified three approaches to women's empowerment : the integrated development approach which focused on women's survival and livelihood needs; the economic development approach which aimed to strengthen women's economic position and the consciousness approach which organized women into collectives that address the sources of oppression.

Adam (1996) argues that empowerment paradigm has replaced of client treatment which dominated social work in former decades. This offers an overview of the challenges and ambiguities of the empowerment paradigm in terms of a wide range of empowering relationships from individuals to communities. It describes self help as the most significant traditional activity in Britain on which empowerment practice draws.

According to Suguna B. (2001) the process of empowerment has provided a broad based activity scheduled to the regional, national and global agencies in which participation has been highlighted. By this method, participation of women in the decision making process could be enhanced many fold and progress attained in a much short time. The process of empowerment helps in identifying areas to be targeted planning strategies for action and outcomes. Empowerment is not a process which is horizontal or vertical but a process which goes round in a circle.

Hill (1990) strongly felt that there is need for a deliberate policy of bringing about occupational diversification by encouraging rural industries and support services.

Verma, S.K. and Saidu Valulla (1991) from their study on self-employed women in Gujarat have observed that the key factors which make the women in the inferior position are poor economic status, limited choice in decision making in financial matters and non-availability of opportunities for participation in money-generating activities.

Rani (1992) conducted a study on potential women entrepreneurs with the objective of exploring the factors that promoted women to start their own business. She found that the desire to do something to be independent was the prime motivating factor, which had influenced women irrespective of their age in setting up their units. Some women viewed entrepreneurship as a tool for earning.

According to Nanavaty Reema (1992) economic empowerment is the basis of social and political empowerment for the poor women. The process of liberation starts only when they are unable to survive the economic and ecological marginalisation through ongoing and local productive work. By their efforts and products they are organized to penetrate and establish a foot hold in the main stream of the economy.

Karl M. (1995) studied the role of empowerment of women on decision making and concluded empowerment as a multifaceted process, involving the pooling of resources to achieve collective strength and countervailing power and entailing and the improvement of manual and technical skills, administrative, managerial and planning capacities and analytical reflective abilities of local women.

According to Pillai J.K. (1995) empowerment is an active, multi-dimensional process, which enables women to realize their full identity and powers in all spheres of life. Power is not a commodity to be transacted nor can it be given away as aims. Power has to be acquired and once acquired, it needs to be exercised, sustained and preserved.

According to Lalitha Rani N. (1996) women form an important segment of the labour force and economic role played by them cannot be isolated from the total framework of development as the role and degree of integration of women in economic development is always an indicator of economic independence and social status.

Choudhary (1996) in her study stressed the need for sharpening women's empowering strategies to make them effective and results oriented. She pointed out that money earned by poor women is more likely to be spent on the basic needs of life than that by men and that this realization would bring women as the focus of development efforts. She also examined the advantages of organizing women groups thereby creating a new sense of dignity and confidence to tackle their problems with a sense of solidarity and to work together for the cause of economic independence.

Carr Marilya, et al.(1997) reviewed women economic empowerment in South Asia. They defined empowerment as the process of challenging existing power relations and of gaining greater control over the sources of the power. Further, the goal of women's empowerment is to challenge patriarchal ideology to transform the structures and institutions that reinforce and perpetuate gender discrimination and social inequality. Empowerment enables poor women to gain access to, and control of, both material and informational resources.

Abdur Rab (1998) examined management of development in growth with equity and stated that the concept of empowerment places emphasis of women's freedom of choice and power to control their own lives at both the personal and social levels. Empowerment is simply gaining the power to make their choice heard to contribute to plans and decisions that affect them to use their expertise at the work to improve their performance and with it the performance of their whole organization.

Jayanthi Ghosh (1998) reported dramatic implications in terms of social interaction within the villages. Even though in Telangana villages (where women constitute the bulk of the paid agriculture workforce) most women have been working outside the home, still membership of the cooperative has greatly increased such outside mobility for women. There is also much more mingling on terms of greater equality as well—between women of different classes, castes and community groups in several of the villages. And most of them felt that they were now in a stronger position within the household especially with regard to financial and economic matters. The most significant change, across the board, seems to be the increase in self-worth and self-assertion of the women concerned.

Ghosh, et al. (1998) conducted research on women entrepreneurs in India and suggested models for their development. He reported that emphasis on economic development without attention to quality of life has resulted in uneven economic growth but not development of societies. The goal of development is not merely to initiate a process of economic growth but also a process, which will improve the lives of people. This implies improvement in the quality of lives of all segments of the population, particularly those groups that have been traditionally marginalized, such as women.

The most comprehensive study on SHGs in Kerala has been the one by Oommen (1999). He covered all the districts and municipalities in the State, in which the Urban Community Development Societies were functioning. The study has reviewed the progress of the programme under four heads : impact on poverty, income-generating programmes, thrift and credit societies and women empowerment. Some of the major findings are about 51 percent of the households investigated are non-poor; housing conditions in Alappuzha and Malappuram have improved to some extent largely through convergence of resources and inputs from different agencies and awareness of various communicable and non-communicable diseases has improved.

Rajeswari and Sumangala (1999) explored the problems and prospects in women entrepreneurship and stated that women entrepreneurship enables to pool the small capital resources and skills available with women. It paves the way for fuller utilization of capital and also mobilizes the female human potential.

Tripathy O.P. (1999) opined that the success of the Indian Self Help Group (SHG) movement has not only helped in realizing the fact that the rural poor are able to save or capable enough to repay, but also open by potential markets for formal financial institutions. It is in this context that the emerging needs of the rural people towards new innovative products of micro-finance should be dealt with serious attention. The winds of change should and must reach the remotest parts of the country, where lies the potential clients of micro-finance.

Bhagya Lakshmi J. (2000) while publishing on some strategic effects towards the empowerment of women stated that the national policy for empowerment of women seeks to adopt an integrated approach towards empowering women through effective convergence of existing services, resources, infrastructure and manpower in both women-specific and women related sectors.

Manimekalai and Jajeswari (2000) reported that the SHG is considered as a viable organization of the rural poor particulary women for delivering micro-credit in order to undertake entrepreneurial activities. Some of the studies of SHGs of the rural poor particulary those managed by women, successfully demonstrated how to mobilize and manage thrift activities, appraise credit needs, enforce financial disciplines, maintain credit linkage with banks and effectively undertake income generating activities etc. The poor as a group are quite creditworthy and repayment of loan is quite satisfactory.

Kalyan (2001) examined resources, agency and achievements, their reflections on the measurement of women empowerment and suggested that emphasis should be given first to make the rural women come out of their domestic set up and to join Self Help Groups. Then according to their needs, interest, skills and feasibility they should be encouraged to undertake the micro enterprise in the concerned field.

Laxmi R.K. (2001) studied Self Help Groups as innovations in financing the poor and revealed that a large number of institutions are at present providing credit to the rural and tribal poor. Yet it is inadequate. The SHGs can create unique alternative, need-based credit delivery mechanisms by pooling their meager resources for catering to their consumption and occupational requirements.

Dogra Bharat (2002) studied women Self Help Groups as kindling spirit of entrepreneurship and examined with the results of many credit programmes. He found that the dissatisfaction with the experiences has demanded new modalities to provide effective financial services to rural poor. Research in various countries have brouth to light the fact that SHGs play a significant role in mobilizing substantial amount of savings.

Prasant Sarangi (2002) observed SHGs in Orissa state and reported that the Self Help Groups (SHGs) in our country have become a source of inspiration for women welfare. Nowadays, formation of SHG is a viable alternative to achieve the objectives of rural development programmes. SHG is also a viable organized set to disburse micro-credit to the rural women and encouraging them to enter into entrepreneurial activities.

An impact study conducted in seven wards with 2003 risk families in Alappuzha by the Department of Statistics, University of Kerala, revealed that families with less than two meals per a day had gone down from 57 percent in 1993 to 49.50 percent in 1996, families with one or more illiterates fell from 26.5 percent to 17.8 percent and families with persons addicted to alcohol declined from 32.5 percent to 22.10 percent.

Punithavathy P. and Eswaran R. (2002) conducted research on empowerment of women through micro-credit and stated that economic empowerment is the initial aspect of women development. The economic empowerment means greater access to financial resources inside and outside the household, reducing vulnerability of poor women to crisis situations like famine, flood, riots death and accidents in the family and significant increase in women's own income. Economic empowerment gives women the power to retain income and use it at her discretion. It provides equal access and control over various resources of the household level. Financial self-reliance of women both in household and in the external environment lead to empowerment of women in other spheres. Micro-credit has resulted in equal access and control over resources at the household level. Micro-credit has resulted in reduced vulnerability of poor women to crisis, famine, floods, riots etc.

Om Raj Sing (2003) analyzed the role of NGOs in fostering Self Help Groups and stated that Self Help Groups are necessary to overcome exploitation, create confidence for the economic self-reliance of rural poor, particularly among women who are mostly invisible in the social structure. These groups enable them to come together for a common objective and gain strength from each other to deal with exploitation. A group becomes the basis for action and change. It also helps building of relationship for mutual trust between the promoting organization and rural poor to constant contact.

The above studies emphasis the need for empowerment of women in order to promote gender equality, to make women as agents of change in society and to increase their capability to enjoy life to the full. Looking at development as freedom and women's issues from the angle of increasing their capabilities are better than concentrating on women's well-being. These studies focus on how women folk can be uplifted through Self Help Groups. It provides an opportunity to improve their financial, social and political status by their involvement as a team. SHGs promote the quality of life by motivating female human potential. In addition, the studies quoted above emphasizes that if women are encouraged to actively involve in SHGs they would exhibit better role responsibilities as an entrepreneur, wife, mother etc. SHG is agreed to be one of the effective means of empowerment of women and thus rural development.

Therefore the preceding review shows that the strategy of micro-financing through SHGs can help in a big way in eradicating poverty and empowering women. However, what is needed is a real change in the community's attitude to depart from the traditional approach of highly subsidized support to the promotion of self help. This is a time consuming process but regular follow up and guidance are sure to bring about substantial improvement.

Studies on Characteristics of Self Help Groups

According to Kumaran K.P. (1991) some of the functions and characteristics of SHGs in Andhra Pradesh are given below :

- Group selects two members as leaders in order to transact their savings and bank accounts, if any.
- Group creates a common fund by contributing a fixed amount by the members on regular period usually once in a month.

- Group meets regularly to discuss their problems, transactions etc.
- The savings generated by the group are either deposited in the bank or rotated among the members as loans for their needs.
- Loans are taken by the members for various purposes.
- Loan amounts are very small and it will be recovered in short time.
- The group collectively or individually takes loan from the bank or from voluntary agency that is in touch with them.
- SHG collectively or individually ensure repayment of above loans.
- NGO helps the SHG in procuring raw materials for income generating projects and also marketing of the produce.
- The loans are decided by the opinion of the group members and the procedure is very simple and flexible.

Gangadhara Rao G. (1995) examines intra-district trends in share, growth and composition of rural non-farm employment (RNFE) of women in West Godavari district for the period 1971-91. The share of RNFE of women increased in delta taluk from 1971 to 1991 whereas it declined in the upland taluk and the agency taluk. At taluk level, Narsapur, Tanuku and Tadepalli Gudem occupied the first three positions among themselves. The growth of RNFE of women in delta and upland taluks was attributed to initial support and vast change in agriculture during 1980s and establishment of female-based agro industries like cashew kernal processing, tobacco handling and fruit juice manufacturing industries. Female employment in delta area was high in household and non-household manufacturing, transport, storage and communication whereas upland area, the female employment was high in construction, trade and commerce. RNFE of female in the district level showed rising trends in all the regions with some discerning differences in growth levels due to agro-economic conditions. Implementation of employment generation programmes by the government and adoption of agro-limatic regional planning approach are the suggestions offered for the removal of disparities on women's earnings.

Anna V. and Pillai N.C. (1990) have found among women entrepreneurs in Kerala, the factors that motivate and compel terms to become entrepreneurs are the ambition to be economically independent, unemployment, encouragement by the State Government and its agencies and success stories of other entrepreneurs. They also observed that most women entrepreneurs liked to start their units in their home town or near home and their choice of trade line was influenced by their convenience.

Rao V.M. (1991) studied promotion of entrepreneurship in Andhra Pradesh and reported that poor financial status of women was found to be very critical in the promotion of entrepreneurship among women. Want of co-operation from family, ignorance about the programmes like DWACRA, IRDP, TRYSEM, insufficient of managerial skills, apathy, sense of fear and high degree of illiteracy, outdated customs and traditions were some of the hindrances on the way of female entrepreneurship. He also found that vast majority of women in the state are interested in organizing Self Help Groups. Women have opted for schemes like fishponds, vegetable cultivation, horticulture, garment shop, petty trade, weaving and breeding mythos to be taken up through SHGs. Financial assistance from the government is required to implement these schemes on an experimental basis. This would go a long way in improving socio-economic status of women.

Alam M.J. (1991) conducted a research on tribal community and examined the role of education on participation of moment in SHGs. He reported that the members of SHGs were unanimous in their opinion that their tribal community wants to secure a place among other communities. To make the necessary requirements they have to take decisions and act diligently to meet the requirements.

Shanthi Kohili (1991) examined women entrepreneurs in India and stated that majority (73 percent) of the members did not attend any entrepreneurial training programme and also they didn't get any financial support from outside. 27 percent are getting financial support from the outside, and 38 percent faced discrimination in business. The majority (63 percent) of them are aware of Government programmes for self-employment.

Rao D.K. (1994) observed SHGs and credit and reported that Group members usually create a common fund by contributing their small savings on a regular basis, group managing pooled resources in a democratic way, consider loan requests and loans are disbursed by purposes. Funds are managed meticulously and there is a far greater responsibility and commitment among the members towards the utilization of the amount for the approved purposes and in repayment. The groups develop their own management system and accountability for handling the resources generated. Moreover local leadership is developed to handle the affairs. The interaction among the members of the group does not restrict itself only to the affairs of savings and loan transaction but often their issues within the group as well as in the community find a forum herein.

A few studies were undertaken by experts like Leela Menon (1994), Lilliana Marulanda (1994) of UNICEF and Sarala Gopalan and Hilda Rajan (1996), all of which were generally uncritical and highly appreciative of the programme. The South Malabar Gramin Bank (1998) conducted a 'Monitoring Study on SHGs' to examine the progress of the scheme since its implementation in 1995-96 in Malappuram and Kozhikode districts. About 60 percent of the bank-linked groups were rated as excellent. In a few groups, group dynamics decreased after the credit linking. The study suggests that in 20 percent of the groups, the organizational setup should undergo change by replacing the existing members. It identified several weaknesses in the Community Development Society (CDS) groups such as lack of monitoring, lack of interest among co-ordinators due to non-receipt of allowance which they had been formerly receiving and static performance of groups.

Kartar Singh and Jain (1995) in their research paper on evolution and survival of SHGs; some theoretical and empirical evidences; explained that there are four stages of group formation: forming, storming, norming, and performing. They identified the factors which have an impact on group formation as full participation of all members, quality in leadership, some sort of homogeneity among the members and transparency in operations and functioning of the groups.

An article by Gramin Vikas (1995) highlights the role of an innovative saving/credit programme called Podupu Lakshmi that had been successfully launched and carried out in the Nellore district of Andhra Pradesh. Podupu Lakshmi is based on a very simple principle of saving a rupee per day/per member. The erstwhile submissive, docile, silent and meek women changed their psyche into assertive, confident, mobile, articulate, questioning and demanding pressure lobby groups. The aspirations of women for economic prosperity went up and they started climbing up the social ladder through the programme. The other factor for the success was the timely intervention of the government machinery. The careful identification of key government functionaries also led to the success of the programme. In Kerala, however, more than nine years have passed since the programme gained momentum.

Gain and Satish (1996) carried out research on the factors affecting groups dynamics and group functioning such as feeling of solidarity and pervasive benefits from group formation, increased awareness of group members, self-reliance and transparency. They feel that dependence on outside source either in material or human terms exist and so the group autonomy is not attained in many cases.

Desai (1997) reported that one of the most basic causes for the women's inferior status is the inadequacy of the legal system to keep pace with the changing needs and times and to provide her with the framework which would enable her to contribute her ability fully to society. Discrimination between sexes may stem from attitudes, customs, traditions and cultural norms. The victims of discrimination look upon law for equality and justice. Law includes not only the provisions of constitution and legislation but also judgments and governmental decisions and actions.

After investigating on women equality and empowerment Jyothi Mitra (1997) found that majority of the (53 percent) respondents participated in their enterprise for 6-8 hours in a day and main motive to start enterprise was to get employment to support family income by using their skills. Their ambition was to get good income and prove good entrepreneurs. They stated that commitment, hard work, efficiency and dedication were the main causes for their success.

Danda (1998) conducted a study on Self Help Groups as an alternative to institutional credit to the poor and found that the credit for consumption is the major purpose in Andhra Pradesh, while it is for social functions and purchase of inputs for agriculture in Karnataka. Petty trade is another reason for which loans are borrowed among the responders. These groups are also linked with banks to undertake income generating activities through which women could achieve economic independence and self-confidence to some extent.

A study by Chowdhary (2000) on reasons for joining SHGs gave rise to nine reasons. They are to avail credit, developing saving habit, to meet unexpected demand for cash, peer pressure, motivated by NGO/Officials, solidarity, exchange of ideas/experiences, attend adult education classes and empowerment. Among all reasons mentioned to avail credit, "to meet unexpected demand for cash" and developing saving habit are prime factors in joining SHGs.

Dasgupta and Rajaram (2001) found that there are many hurdles involved in the process for promoting micro enterprises through SHGs. The attempt is worth one and the sustained efforts by the Government, NGOs and SHGs in the long run can generate huge employment opportunities among the rural women and thus eradicate poverty among the rural masses.

According to Jha (2001) Micro Finance provides credit access to poor with no collateral obligations. It encourages savings and promotes income-generating activities. Loans are provided at the market driven rates of interest and peer pressure is used in repayment. Micro Finance is carried out through Self Help Groups, where poor come together in the range of 10-20 by weekly, fortnightly and monthly meetings through their savings and loaning. It is hoped that through such interventions hitherto uncovered groups are covered with credit and in the process get empowered.

According to Lakshmi R. Kulshresta (2001) stated that experience has shows that many of the poverty alleviation programmes through organized credit channels have not achieved that required success. It has been observed that in respect of financing poverty alleviation programmes and creation of employment in rural areas there are a number of factors which prevent small borrowers and poor people from securing adequate credit from formal credit agency, such as lack of awareness among beneficiaries in respect of development through credit and there by making proper use of credit.

Madheswaran S. and Amita Dharmadhikary (2001) reported that most of the loans taken by the members of SHGs are for agricultural activity followed by petty business, allied activities, medicine, family need, marriage and house building. It has also been observed that poorer the members, less is the diversification of the loans.

Panth S. and Ananth (2001) stated that one of the drawbacks of self help employment programme is their concentration on the inputs, rather than output (finished products) and marketing of products. To ratify this situation, Swarna Jayanti Gram Swarojar Yojana provides avenues for promotion of marketing of the goods product by the rural self help groups.

Archana Gupta (2001) reported that a typical tribal women's SHGs performs a number of functions such as enabling members to become self dependent and self reliant, providing a forum for members for discussing their socio-economic problems, developing decision making capacity and leadership qualities among members and equipping women with the basic skill required for understanding monetary transactions.

Regarding working pattern of Self Help Groups, Archana Sinha (2002) revealed that SHGs collect the deposits from their members and lend to the needy members for production purposes and also for subsistence and consumption needs. It takes loans from banks or voluntary agencies or self help promoting institutions to meet the needs of the members. SHG itself with the help of NGO makes assessment of individual credit needs of its members and submits to the bank for sanction of collective loans in its name. NGO helps the SHG in procuring raw materials and also marketing of the produce. SHG collectively ensure repayment of bank loans. Entire loan amount disbursed to SHGs is refinanced by NABARD to the financing bank.

Further, she stated that groups generate a common fund where each member contribute his/her savings on a regular basis. Groups meet periodically to discuss their transactions, loans are decided by consensus. Loans cover a variety of purposes including non-traditional ones also. Loan amounts are small and for short duration, loan procedure is very simple and flexible, defaults are negligible and groups are mobilizing savings from their members and are effectively rotating the same among their members.

It is necessary that Self Help Groups and Micro Credit should be seen as one of the components of a solution to accelerate the socio-economic development particularly of the rural poor women in India. A judicious mix of Micro Credit along with other activities with emphasis on development and empowerment strategies and processes would certainly make Micro Credit an effective instrument of social and economic development particularly of the women in a holistic and integrated manner.

According to D'Silva (2001) though women are organized into Self Help Groups possessing huge corpus contributing to socio-economic development of the district is very low hence unable to take up production activities on large scale.

According to Kumaran K.P. (2001) some of the functions and characteristics of SHGs in Andhra Pradesh are given below :

- Group selects two members as leaders in order to transact their savings and bank accounts if any.
- Group creates a common fund by contributing a fixed amount by the members on regular period usually once in a month.
- Group meets regularly to discuss their problems, transactions etc.
- The savings generated by the group are either deposited in the Bank or rotated among the members as loans for their needs.
- Loans are taken by the members for various purposes.
- Loan amounts are very small and it will be recovered in short time.

- The group collectively or individually takes loan form the Bank or from voluntary agency who is in touch with them in generating activities.
- SHG collectively or individually ensure repayment of above loans.
- NGO helps the SHG in procuring raw materials for income generating projects and also marketing of the produce.
- The loans are decided by the opinion of the Group members and the procedure is very simple and flexible.

Awasthi P. et al. (2002), explored the working and impact of Self Help Groups on economic status of women in watershed areas of Madhya Pradesh and pointed out that the SHG members suffered from lack of motivation, backward and forward linkages, inadequate provision for marketing and availability of inputs, lack of systematic monitoring and follow-up of the activities.

Kumaran K.P. (2002) examined the experiences in SHGs in promoting micro-enterprise through Micro Credit intervention. The study was conducted in the Pune district of Maharashtra State. 15 sample cases of SHGs were selected on a random basis. Among them 10 groups were promoted jointly by NGO and Bank. While the remaining five of them were formed by District Rural Development Agency (DRDA). From the selected SHGs, 90 members were interviewed to study the structure and operation of SHGs. Further, 29 entrepreneurs selected from the group were interviewed to study in detail the promotion, functioning and sustainability of micro-enterprises. He reported that due to technical training and escort services provided to the entrepreneurs, the micro-enterprises set up by the members of the SHGs promoted by NGO and banks were more viable and sustainable as compared to those formed by the DRDA promoted groups, where these services were lacking.

Rao V.M. (2002) examined empowerment of farm women through dairy cooperatives in Andhara Pradesh and stated that the SHGs collect the deposits from their members and lend to the needy members for production purposes and also for subsistence and consumption needs. It takes loans from banks or voluntary agencies or self help promoting institutions to meet the needs of the members. SHG itself with the help of NGO make assessment of individual credit needs of its members and submits to the bank for sanction of collective loans in its name. NGO helps the SHG in procuring raw material and also marketing of the produce. SHG collectively ensures repayment of bank loans. Entire loan amount disbursed to SHGs is refinanced by NABARD to the financing bank.

It could be noticed from the above studies that an ideal SHG should frame and abide by certain rules to be strictly followed for the success of it. By being a member of SHG there is possibility for better participation, decision making, planning for future etc. There is a need to equip them in developing management skills especially in financial issues.

Studies on Effects of Self Help Groups

Jyothi Rani and Prabhakar (1990) studied the impact of dairying scheme on living conditions of scheduled castes. They reported an improvement in the living conditions particulary in terms of food in all the sample beneficiaries. The progress has also been noticed in other aspects like clothing, education, health, reduction in debts, improvement in agriculture etc. However the positive effect on the living conditions of small farmers was high compared to marginal farmers.

Chatterjee and Meera (1990) conducted a study on rural and tribal women in India; their health and economic productivity. They conducted their study in Maharashtra with 239 families. Above 64 families were involved in SHGs. They found that mothers who are participating in Self Help Groups are having better awareness about children's health care, better understanding about family planning programmes than the women who did not participate in SHGs.

Srinivasan L. (1990) reported that SHGs provided women an opportunity to meet together, identified and communicate their problems, exchange experiences and development forums of solidity and mutual assistance. More over this collective work has allowed women to increase their self-esteem and to plan, question and organize to confront inequality at both public and personal levels.

According to Panandiker S. (1991) problems and prospects of self-employed women and reported that as women have to play dual role, self-employment is better suited to them. If she is the authority of her enterprise she can have her own timings and adjustments.

A study by Savitha Singal and Kamala Srinivasan (1991) observed rural women's participation in paid work their satisfaction and felt needs and found that in Hissar District of Haryana revealed that women earned higher income both economically as well as psychologically through self-employment than wage employment. They perceived better say in family decisions and more respect from their husband.

Alam M.J. (1991) conducted a study on education and participation of women in Self Help Groups in Bihar. He examined the means of recreation and daily way of their life and reported that women who are participating in Self Help Groups are able to develop their own methods for education of their children. They are able to relate the education to their folklore songs, riddles, proverbs as means of recreation and daily way of life.

Ramanan J. (1992) conducted a study on the financial independence of mothers (N = 189) from low income families. In comparison to mothers who were not employed, employed mothers scored higher on a mental aptitude test. Financial status of mother was also associated with measures of the current family functioning. There was less poverty and higher home environment scores when mothers were employed. Hierarchical multiple regressions showed that children's academic achievement was positively predicted by maternal employment depending on the types of non-maternal care to which children are exposed but unfortunately this issue has not been explored empirically. The evidence available thus demonstrates that contrary to popular belief maternal employment does not necessarily have harmful effects on child development. In fact, many of the effects may be beneficial.

Ghosh D.K. (1992) cited that women themselves change fundamentally when they are members of a strong functional women's group. This results because difference between weakness and strength lies in well built cohesive organization. These changes at the feeling level are integrally linked with experiences of successful collective action and result in changes in status and self-concept of women.

Studies on self help group by Prem Kumar and Rahul Mehta (1992) reviewed the success or failure of development projects and also how far the families are benefitted by the programme. All the beneficiaries had crossed the poverty line with an additional income ranging from 280 to 395 by participating in SHGs thus improving their socio-economic status.

Mahajan V.S. (1993) conducted a survey on sustainable development of women in Maharashtra and found that the women in group activities significantly contributed in improving their self-confidence. Communication skills are improved after association with SHGs. The members were relatively more assertive confronting social evils and problem situations. A fall in incidence of family violence was evident.

Singh (1994) examined management of common pool resources among women cooperatives and pointed out that cooperation emerges when it either reduced the cost and or increased the benefits to the prospective members from undertaking an activity of common interest. So long as these requirements are met it is likely that the members would not abandon cooperation and the cooperative will survive and prosper.

Syngal B.S. (1994) proved from his studies that the greater participation of women can ensure increased membership increased paid up share capital and increased deposits, increased turnover and business viability and devoted and loyal membership. In rural areas some societies gave training in handicrafts and cottage industries, have been organized. But on the whole women continued to play a insignificant role in the development of the cooperative sector. Women in cooperatives can increase paid up share capital and deposits, improve turnover and business viability and provide a devoted and loyal membership to the cooperative societies.

The study conducted by Karkar (1995) revealed that as the SHG programme was effectively implemented, the monthly income of the beneficiaries had increased substantially. A large number of groups had become mini-banks reducing the dependence on moneylenders. It had also resulted in improving their standards of hygiene and nutrition. The major findings were that the urge for literacy especially for the girl child and the adoption of family planning measures had increased. The process of group dynamics strengthened the networking, homogeneity and self-esteem of women. The "we can do it" syndrome is a part of their psyche today. The scheme had also provided women the opportunity to sit together, discuss and share their long pending problems and seek joint solutions through sympathetic cooperation and advice. The group thus acts both as a pillar of strength and an information window.

Agnihotri (1995) examined self-employment and entrepreneurship development programmes among rural and tribal women and observed the impact of SHGs on socio-economic status of rural and tribal women in Khanora. Nearly 150 families (women) were interviewed for the study and he found that the women of Khanora were strongly determined to change their socio-economic status. They were able to procure enough food, clothing and better shelter.

Gopalakrishnan B.K. (1996) stated that the self help group (SHG) is a mini voluntary agency for self help at the micro level has been a focus on the weaker sections particularly women for their social defense. SHG has got great potential in creating awareness on day affairs, promoting savings habit, developing self and community assets, increasing income level, improving social power etc. SHG and Bank linkage has improved their credit worthiness and repaying capacity. This can contribute economic development, child education, health and sanitation etc. through women. No doubt SHGs will replace commercial/co-operative lending institutions and the villages or at least supplement rural financing. SHG concept generates self-confidence, self-security and self-reliance.

Lalitha Rani N. (1996) conducted a study on women empowerment through cooperatives and found that in India in general poor rural women in particular are relatively powerless with little or no control over resources and little decision making power. Often decision made by others affects their lives. The prevail patriarchal ideology which promotes the values of submission, sacrifice, obedience and silent suffering often undermines even these attempts by women to assert themselves or demand some share of resources. From the study she proved that pre-requisite to promote empowerment of women in rural areas is promotion of organizing among women. Women can be organized through a variety of means namely through formation of cooperatives, Mahila Mandals and self help groups.

Kumaran K.P.S. (1997) explored self help groups as an alternative to credit system to the poor in Andhra Pradesh and revealed that credit for consumption is the major purpose in Andhra Pradesh while its social functions and purchase of inputs for agriculture are in Karnataka. Petty trade is another reason for which loans are borrowed among all the respondents. These groups are also linked with banks to undertake income generating activities through which women could achieve economic independence and self-confidence to some extent.

Ghosh Paul D. (1998) researched the effect of entrepreneurship on women in India and found that SHGs have obtained the necessary skills to produce a product, manage funds, organize the operation of enterprise and main decision. These activities link them to the market, government departments, public etc., from which these women located previously. Self-employment has thus improved their position in the home and in the community.

Narasani Laxmi (1998) examined the role of banking in rural development and stated that the SHG linkage programme has mostly highlighted the economic criteria. The awareness on the SHGs have created and the attitudinal changes they have brought in the minds and outlook of the members have definitely helped in realizing their own intrinsic strength. Formation of groups with homogeneous background and interest which is key to the success of the credit linkage programme gradually leads to a situation where self help groups transcend economic issues and are induced to take up other related issues.

Shylendra (1998) attempted to evaluate the performance of eight women SHGs promoted in the Vidaj village by the Institute of Rural Management (IRM), Anand. Here the SHGs failed to enable members to realize their potential benefits. The reasons identified for the failure were the wrong approach followed in the SHG formation by the team, misconceptions about SHG goals both among the team and the members and lack of clarity about the concept. The main lessons drawn from the project are the need for creating SHGs based on a clear assessment of the needs of different sections of the society, ensuring clear understanding of the concept of SHG among team members involved in promoting SHGs and enhancing the relevance of SHGs to their members by enabling them to meet effectively their requirements be it savings or credit or income generating activities.

Tirupati (1998) conducted a study on women in India, involvement in self-employment and its impact on development of women and he found that women respondents experienced sense of achievement and improved in their earnings. Their skills of public relations are also improved than before.

Mohan Rao R.M. and Appa Rao, C.H. (1999) studied women Self Help Groups in Andhra Pradesh and found that the highest rate of tangible benefits is derived by SHGs than DWCRA members. The members of SHGs are enjoying the fruits of saving by improving their skills in different areas like Tailoring, Painting, Embroidering, Soft Toys Making and they are occupying themselves in different self-employment like vegetable selling, pickle making, basket weaving and traditional craft works.

Devada (1999) examined economic development of Indian women and stated that women's participation in self help groups is believed to increase their status and decision making power. Employed women do not remain as objects of social change but became agents of it. Similar results were found by Aggarwal J.C. and Aggarwal S.P. (1999). According to them SHGs create awareness among the parents to send their children to the school and also provide training for the women to become Balwadi teachers.

Thangamuthu and Manimekalai (1999) carried out a survey on generation of employment for women through self help groups. They reported that the beneficiaries had crossed the poverty line with additional income of Rs. 255/- to Rs. 460/-. The problems faced by the beneficiaries in their trades were scarcity of raw material and difficulty in marketing.

Basu Kishanjit and Jindal Krishnan (2000) stated that the Indian micro finance scene is dominated by self help groups (SHGs) and their linkage to banks. The Indian development is unique for its use of formal institutions in providing finance to SHGs instead of creating parallel non-formal channels of routing finance to poor. The plan of link 2,00,000 groups has brought to therefore the issues at group formation and nurturing before linkage with banks. Innovative forms of financing are therefore to be developed which are based on sound commercial principles and yet help to alleviate poverty. Credit delivery through thrift and credit groups (self help groups) emerge as an alternative to the existing system of credit disbursement by the banks.

Gurumoorthy T.R. (2000) stated that the SHG aim at providing awareness among the poor about the non-going development programmes. The poor should know how best to use existing government programmes and also the legal provisions meant for the disadvantage sections of the rural communities.

Khan S.S. (2000) stated a woman entrepreneur can start an enterprise at a small scale. There are a number of women entrepreneurs who have started small enterprises but later expanded them to large scale units. For instance, Ms. Shahnaz Hussain, president of CIDESCO hailing from Kailash has placed Indian herbals in the world cosmetic map. She started with an investment of just Rs. 35,000/-. A women self help group in Dindigul District runs a unit providing agro-services with the total turnover crossing Rs. 12 lakhs per annum.

Kumaran et al. (2000) examined the impact of SHGs on women and their studies concluded that SHGs helped in improving socio-economic conditions of their members. Major factors which helped SHGs are socio-economic homogeneity of the group, small size of the family, functionality, participation, voluntary mode, non-political nature and above all similarities of needs and problems of group members.

Ramalakshmi C.S. (2000) hgihlights the role of an innovative saving/credit programme called Podupu Lakshmi that had been successfully launched and carried out in Nellore district of Andhra Pradesh. She noticed that Podupu Lakshmi is based on a very simple principle of saving a rupee per day/per member. The erstwhile submissive, docile, silent and meek women changed their psyche into assertive, confident, mobile, articulate, questioning and demanding pressure lobby groups. The aspirations of women for economic prosperity went up and they started climbing up the social ladder through the programme. The other factor for the success was the timely intervention of the government machinery. The careful identification of key government functionaries also led to the success of the programme.

Her study on DWCRA as a successful experiment to emancipate rural women in Andhra Pradesh and concluded that with the support from the Government of Andhra Pradesh, the rural women have now transformed their lives into full time and active entrepreneurs with lot of hope and are able to lead a life with self-esteem. Once they were passive recipients of Governments dolbs, but now they are active participants and stake holders in the programmes. They have risen to the levels of self-management. They have realized the importance of their numbers and have become capable of asking for their rights/entitlements like equal wages, better working conditions, health, education, nutrition for their children, etc. Thus DWCRA has become a powerful tool in bringing women together in the remote rural areas and thus helped to emancipate the once mute sufferers in silence to march forward towards collective community progress/development on a substantial basis.

Jha, (2001) stated that some of the benefits of women's SHGs are inculcation of spirit of self-effort and self-reliance among women, enabling a forum for women to exchange ideas and experiences, providing opportunities to women in productive work, foresting spirit of cooperation among women promoting awareness, providing opportunities to acquire skills and instilling confidence.

Laxmi R.K. (2001) reported that SHGs are to supplement credit strategies for meeting the needs of the poor by combining the flexibility, sensitivity and responsiveness of the informal credit system with the technical/administrative capabilities and financial resources of formal financial institutions to build mutual trust and confidence between bankers and the tribal poor and to encourage banking in a segment of population that formal financial institution usually find difficult to reach this innovative form of financing is imperative.

Archana Gupta (2001) explored SHG as an innovation in financing the poor and found that small savings by rural women can generate the requisite resources which can wean the people away from the exploitation of money lenders. Savings depend on habits and voluntary savings constitute the key for economic progress. It has also been provided that poor people can save substantially through group efforts. Promotion of self help groups have the potential development paving the way for sustainable development. She concluded that the SHGs aim at providing awareness among the poor about the ongoing development programmes. The poor should know how best to use existing government programmes and also the legal provisions meant for the disadvantaged sections of the rural communities.

Jayaramana (2002) stated that government and NGOs have encouraged women to start micro-enterprise. Any small enterprise that involves the investment at about Rs. 50,000 could be considered as a micro-enterprise. These micro-enterprises are sought to be promoted by the Self Help Groups (SHGs). SHGs are recognized to stay as the reliable forum for savings and credit.

Kokila K. (2002) examined DWCRA bazaar as a successful experiment in Andhra Pradesh. She reported that the DWCRA bazaar is yet another advance step in the process of empowerment of women and helps members to get an exposure to marketing concepts, better technology, increased productivity and provides an opportunity to interface with consumers resulting in increased self-esteem of these women.

Studies have shown that the delivery of micro finance to the poor is smooth, effective and less costly if they are orgnized into Self Help Groups (SHG). Kumaran's study (2002) is primarily intended to document the experiences in SHGs in promoting micro enterprises through micro credit intervention. This study was conducted in Pune district of Maharashtra state. 15 sample cases of SHGs were selected on a random basis. Among them 10 groups were promoted jointly by NGO and Bank, while the remaining five of them were formed by District Rural Development Agency (DRDA). From the selected SHGs 90 members were interviewed to study the structure and operation of SHG. Further, 29 entrepreneurs selected from the group were interviewed to study in detail the promotion, functioning and sustainability of micro enterprise. He reported that due to technical training and escort services provided to the entrepreneurs, the micro enterprises set up by the members of the SHGs promoted by NGO and banks were more viable and sustainable as compared to those formed by the DRDA promoted group where these services was lacking.

Singh Mor D.P. (2002) stated that initiatives and constitutional and legislative provisions for the empowerment of women have focused upon qualitative changes in education, health and empowerment. The removal of gender inequality is based upon the redistribution of social power and a change in the control of resources in favour of women.

Vashitha K.C., Malik and Sashi (2002) reported that there are many instances where SHGs have successfully taken up group causes and fought against deprivations and social stigmas. While successfully playing their predetermined role in economic empowerment the SHGs have also begun to play a role as vehicles of social progress. Rural women are less endowed than men with education, health care or productive assets and financial resources. Finance, being an entry point to rural development, non-accessibility and non-availability of credit to rural women have been instrumental in aggravating gender inequalities in the rural areas. Financial resources, if effectively delivered to women can help them make a meaningful improvement in their economic and social conditions.

Sebastian T. (2002) pointed out that the SHG members suffered from lack of motivation, backward and forward linkages, inadequate provision for marketing and availability of inputs, lack of systematic monitoring and follow up of the activities. The government and NGOs have thought it fit to encourage women to start micro-enterprises. The rural women have shown that they are creditworthy and can handle money responsibility and work as teams.

Dwarakanath H.D. (2002) conducted a study on rural credit and women self help groups in Ranga Reddy district in Andhra Pradesh taking ten cooperative thrift and credit societies. These Banks collectively enrolled 2090 SH groups covering 28,579 women members and deposited a share capital of rupees one crore and mobilized Rs. 319 crores from thrift deposits. About 5000 self help groups were sanctioned loan component worth Rs. 13.39 lakhs for the year 2001-2002 with a subsidy of Rs. 7.5 lakhs covering 85 per cent beneficiaries belonging to weaker sections of the society. It is interesting to note that the Sneha Mahila Bank of Medchal stands first in the district with a thrift deposit of Rs. 8.7 lakhs covering about 300 self help groups comprising 3032 women members. About 178 women groups availed loan facilities worth Rs. 23.45 lakhs from the Bank. Similarly Gandveed Mahila Bank advanced loans worth Rs. 11.15 lakhs, followed by Maheswaram Bank Rs. 11.13 and Kesara Bank with Rs. 9.17 lakhs loan component.

Chiranjeevi T. (2003) conducted a study on empowering women through SHG and found that women have developed abundant self-confidence and self-esteem through SHGs movement. Not only economic poverty but also social and gender issues can be tackled effectively through this process.

Prasant Sarangi (2003) stated that women lead SHGs in many parts of the country have achieved success in bringing the women to the mainstream of decision making. SHGs are also available organized setup to disburse micro credit to the rural women and encourage them to enter into entrepreneurial activities. The women lead self help groups in village of Purushottampur block of Ganjam district of Orissa state have successfully demonstrated how to mobilize and manage thrift appraise credit needs, maintain linkage with the banks and enforce financial self discipline.

Studies quoted above emphasizes that if women are encouraged to actively involve in SHGs they would exhibit better role responsibilities as an entrepreneur, wife, mother etc. Women groups have proved that they would indeed bring about a sea change in the mindset of the very conservative and traditional bound illiterate women in rural areas. These groups as a viable alternative to achieve the objectives of rural development and to set community participation with economic power and potentialities proved that with the help of district administration and local officials they could indeed bring in socio-economic development to enhance their self employment potential. Hence, SHG is agreed to be one of the effective means of empowerment of women and thus rural development.

3

METHODOLOGY

The introduction of self help groups has been a recent and a revolutionary change in the economic structure of our country. Since independence India is suffering from severe socio-economic problems. Poverty has become a major threat to the economic development of our country. Therefore the planners and policy makers thought of identifying certain avenues and measures to check the wide spread poverty. One such solution is the formation of self help group (SHG). In the name itself it is clear that these groups are formed to help by themselves. The role of SHG is very significant in present day context both in motivating women to save at least some money regularly and to use that amount as investment in some income generating activities.

As is evident, poverty has remained the vulnerable challenge in India's development efforts to bring about a perceptible change in the quality of life of its teeming millions. India, being a developing country, a vast section of its population suffer from malnutrition, unemployment and poor health care. This is particularly true in the case of main weaker sections of society namely women, children, scheduled castes and scheduled tribes.

In rural India, the high rate of illiteracy and low economic status of women underline the need to accelerate their earning power by providing the income generating assets. Provisions of employment opportunities and income to rural women is one way to improve their nutrition, health, education and social status. In most of the developing countries greater emphasis is laid on the imperative need for development of rural women and their active involvement in the mainstream of development. In our country continuous efforts are being made by the union and state governments to improve the status of rural women, especially those below the poverty line through different schemes of rural development.

Ever since independence a number of innovative schemes have been launched for the upliftment of women in our country. There has been a perceptible shift from viewing women as critical agents for socio-economic development. Now the emphasis has shifted from development to empowerment.

Women constitute one half of the segment of pluralism in India. The 1991 census counted 407.1 million females against a total population of 846.3 million in which 207.8 million women live in rural areas and 27 percent of the rural women live below the poverty line. Enhancing women's economic productivity is an important strategy for improving the welfare of 60 million Indian households living below the poverty line. Hence, the emphasis is stressed on the empowerment of rural women focusing on the following aspects.

- Direct involvement of women in programming and management.
- Effective collaboration with community organisations.
- Organising and strengthening of women's self help groups (SHGs).
- Sensitisation and advocacy of Gender Just Society.
- Organising women in different groups to undertake certain productive activities to earn their livelihood and to develop rural community.

Need and Importance of the Study

Empowerment is closely linked to economic independence. Nothing succeeds better than the power of self help. And when efforts are supported by the private organisations the results could be extremely gratifying. Today self help groups of women in Andhra Pradesh focussed around economic activities like savings, collective marketing, promotion of individual enterprise and in the process moving into the mainstream of society. In the process, leadership qualities blossom, discipline prevails and the true democracy begins to function. This also helps add value to the work they do, to their families and their communities. A heartening fact is that 50 percent of such self help groups in the country have been formed in Andhra Pradesh alone.

A social movement has thus begun wherein rural women started saving money by forming themselves into small groups and came together to decide all issues which effect their life. During the last five-six years saving movement caught up the imagination of women as a mean of self help groups through which they are trying to mould their destiny. The introduction of self help groups has been a recent revolutionary phenomenon in the economic structure of our country. Even since independence India is facing severe socio-economic problems. Poverty has become a major threat to the economic development of our country. Therefore the planners and policy makers thought of identifying certain avenues and measures to check the widespread poverty. One such solution is the formation of self help groups (SHGs). The very name indicates that these groups are formed to help by themselves. The role of self help groups is very significant in the present day context both in motivating women to save at least some money regularly and to use that amount as investment in income generating activities. Thus it may be rated as the most successful anti-poverty programmes. Since so much is being said about the programme and contribution to women's empowerment and the expectation continue to be high, the need for taking a look at the present status has been felt. Thus women empowered by economic independence can contribute to society and at the same time improve their standard of living and self esteem can be demonstrated and taken to logical end where an empowered womenfolk will take their right full place in the path of progress.

The government of Andhra Pradesh has taken up the theme of Women's employment as one of the main agenda items to tackle rural poverty through social mobilisation. Self help group (SHG) movement through savings has been taken up by the department of Panchayat Raj and Rural Development to mould the social life of the rural women. Andhra Pradesh is the pioneer state to introduce self help group concept to achieve self sufficiency and to bring social transformation among the rural women living below poverty line. Over 30 lakh women belonging to the weaker sections of the society have become members of these self help groups.

Ever since the inception, self help groups are making great strides in the country and Andhra Pradesh stands foremost in ranking with 3,73,044 Self Help Groups in 1999-2000 and the number of SHGs increased to 4,36,579 in 2002-2003 and non-governmental organisations are doing Yeomen service in motivating women to form into self help groups.

Hence, the present project titled "Empowerment of Rural Women Through Self Help Groups : A study in Chittoor district of Andhra Pradesh" has been embarked.

Objectives of the Study

The following are the main objectives of the present study :

- To analyse the role of self help groups in the social, economic and political empowerment of women.
- To study the socio-economic profile of the self help group members.

- To study the functioning of self help groups.
- To assess the extent of awareness regarding the governmental programmes.
- To study the nature of participation of women in self help groups.
- To examine and evaluate the specific problems of beneficiaries with regard to savings, revolving fund, productivity, marketing etc.

Hypothesis

The following specific hypotheses have been formulated to meet the above objectives of the study :

- Self Help Groups (SHGs) leads to economic empowerment of women.
- Economic empowerment of beneficiaries leads to social empowerment in the form of better nutrition, health and general awareness.
- Self Help Groups helps in promoting leadership qualities among the beneficiaries.
- Self Help Groups which is part and parcel of rural life is a good means for empowerment.

Methodology

Keeping in view the specific set of objectives enumerated, an in-depth study of self help groups in Chittoor district of Andhra Pradesh has been selected. In this regard methodology needs special emphasis. The study is based on collection of data from both primary and secondary sources in the district of Chittoor in Andhra Pradesh.

Sampling Design

The sampling design is formulated for the purpose of collection of primary data. Chittoor district in Rayalaseema region of Andhra Pradesh is selected purposively for the following reasons :

- Chittoor district experienced a spurt in non-governmental organisations and self help groups.

This district stands unique with regard to promotion of self help groups.

- Chittoor district is one of the backward districts of Andhra Pradesh state in terms of the levels of female literacy, female employment and other socio-economic parameters.
- Familiarity and proximity of the district makes convenient for conduct of the study.

Chittoor district forms the southern most part of Andhra Pradesh. It is one of the four drought-prone districts of the Rayalaseema region of Andhra Pradesh. The district is divided into three Revenue divisions namely Chittoor, Tirupati and Madanapalli and is further divided into sixty six Mandals covering one thousand four hundred and eighty five villages.

At the time of sample selection *i.e.* in the year 2000 there were one thousand nine hundred and forty self help groups functioning in the district. Out of them one thousand one hundred and thirty were in Tirupati Division, three hundred and ninety were in Chittoor Division and four hundred and twenty were in Madanapalli Division. At present there are 32,341 self help groups functioning in the district.

Multistage cluster stratified sampling method was adopted for collecting primary data by designing the sample from population. Self Help Groups are functioning in almost all the Mandals of Chittoor District. Since it is not possible to cover all the Mandals in this inquiry and to keep the study within manageable limits without in any way minimizing its significance twelve Mandals (at the rate of four Mandals from each revenue division) have been selected for the study. They are :

Tirupati Revenue Division

- Renigunta
- Srikalahasthi

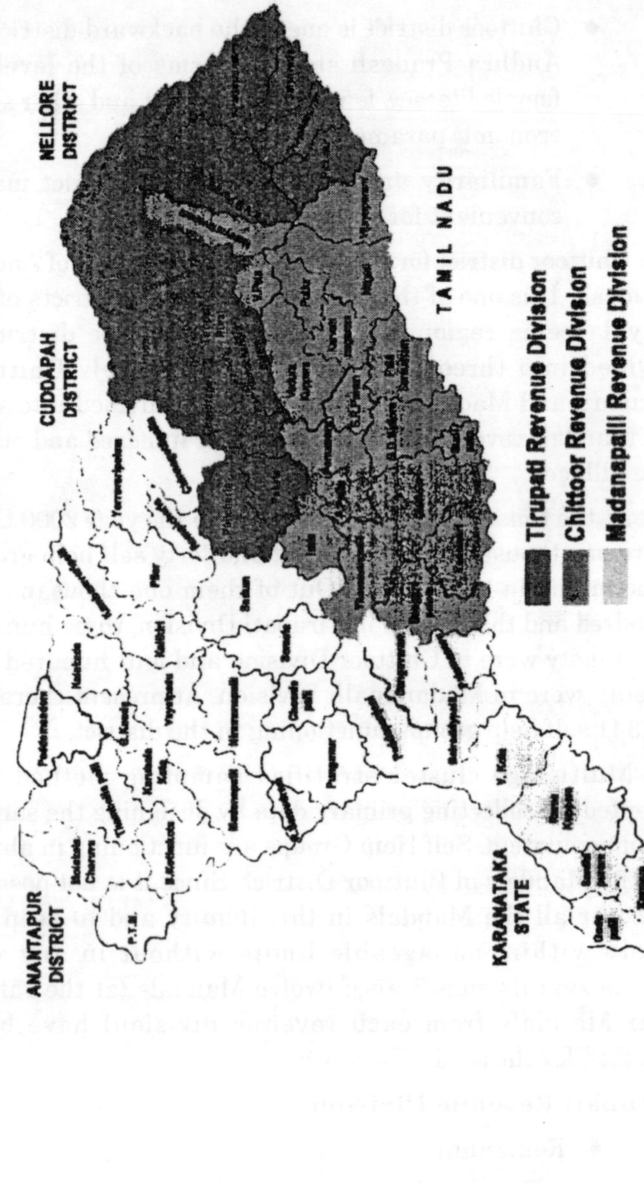

Selected Three Revenue Divisions of Chittoor District

ANANTAPUR DISTRICT

CUDDAPAH DISTRICT

NELLORE DISTRICT

TAMIL NADU

KARANATAKA STATE

Tirupati Revenue Division

Chittoor Revenue Division

Madanapalli Revenue Division

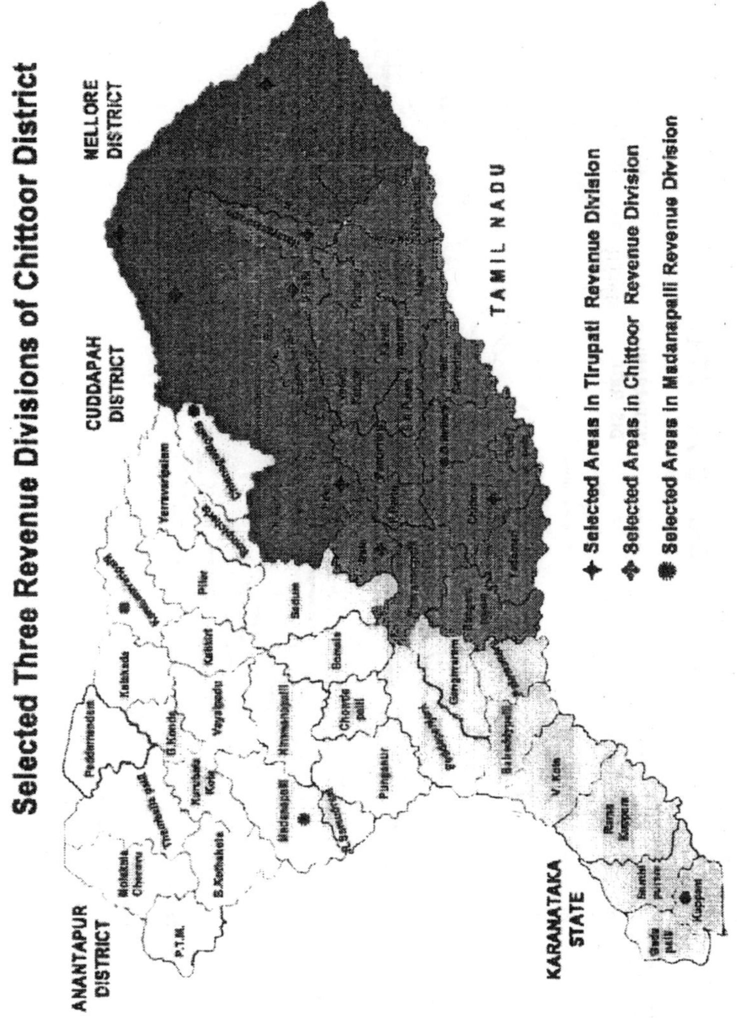
Selected Three Revenue Divisions of Chittoor District
ANANTAPUR DISTRICT
CUDDAPAH DISTRICT
NELLORE DISTRICT
TAMIL NADU
KARANATAKA STATE
Selected Areas in Tirupati Revenue Division
Selected Areas in Chittoor Revenue Division
Selected Areas in Madanapalli Revenue Division

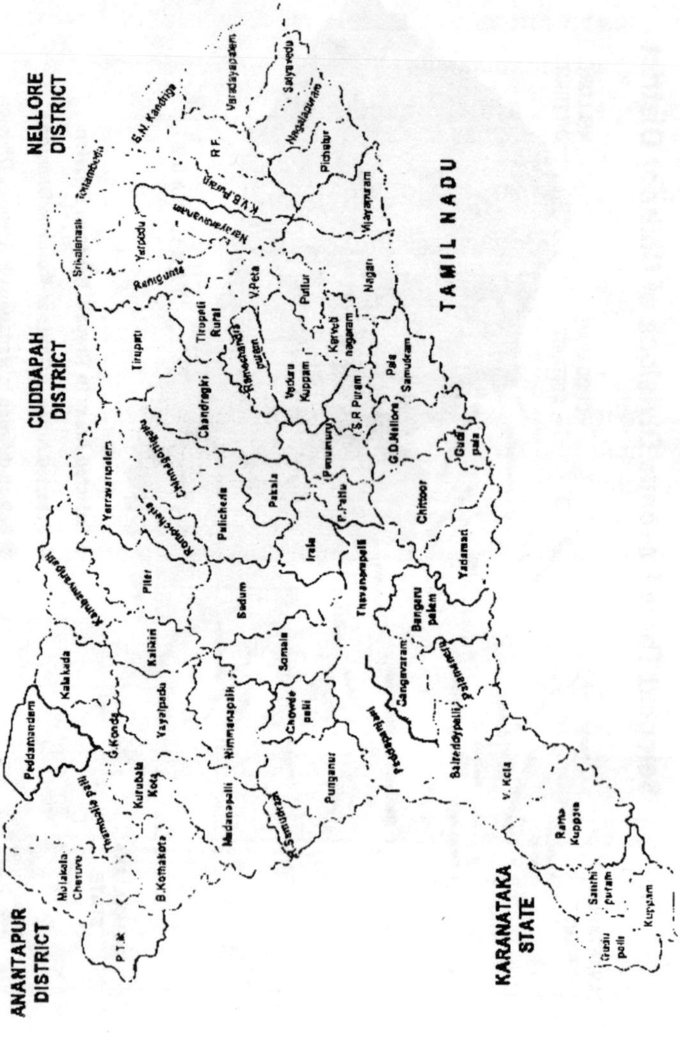

MAP OF CHITTOOR DISTRICT

- Pakala
- Varadaiahpalem

Chittoor Revenue Division

- Chittoor
- Vadamalpet
- Narayanavanam
- Irala

Madanapalli Revenue Division

- Chinnagottigallu
- Madanapalli
- K.V. Palli
- Kuppam

With in the study area again five panchayats from each Mandal and five villages from each Panchayat have been selected. A total sample of 300 beneficiaries (at the rate of 100 sample from each revenue division) has been selected. The schematic Research Sampling Design is presented in the following table 1 & 2.

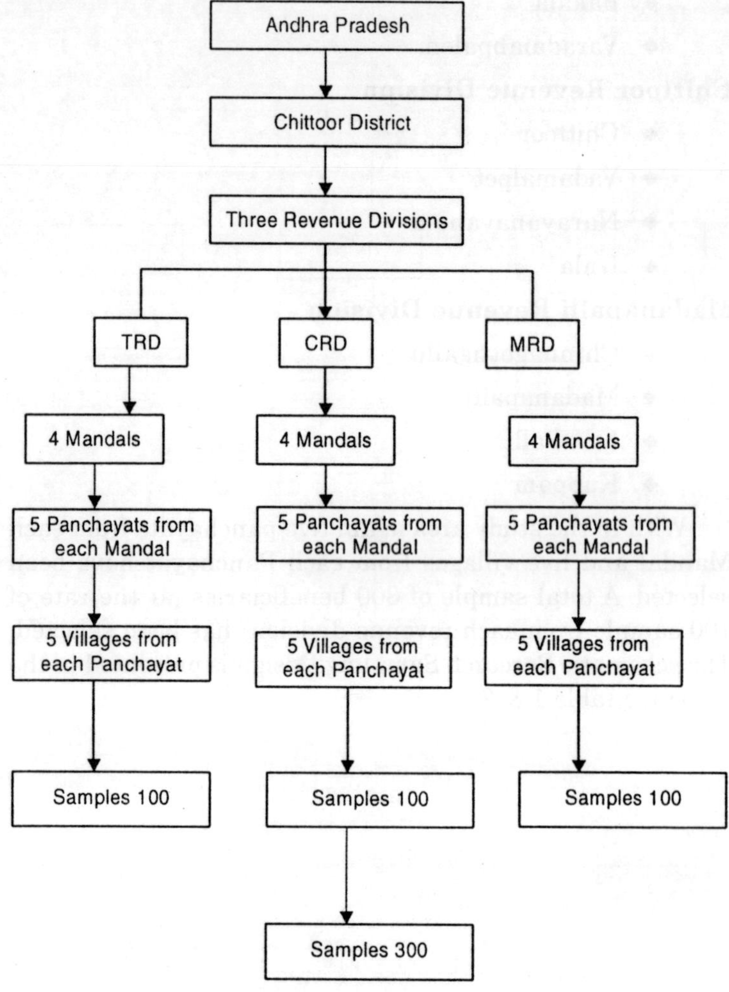

TRD : Tiruapti Revenue Division.
CRD : Chittor Revenue Division.
MRD : Madanapalli Revenue Division.

Fig.—3.2

Schematic Research Design of Sample Selection

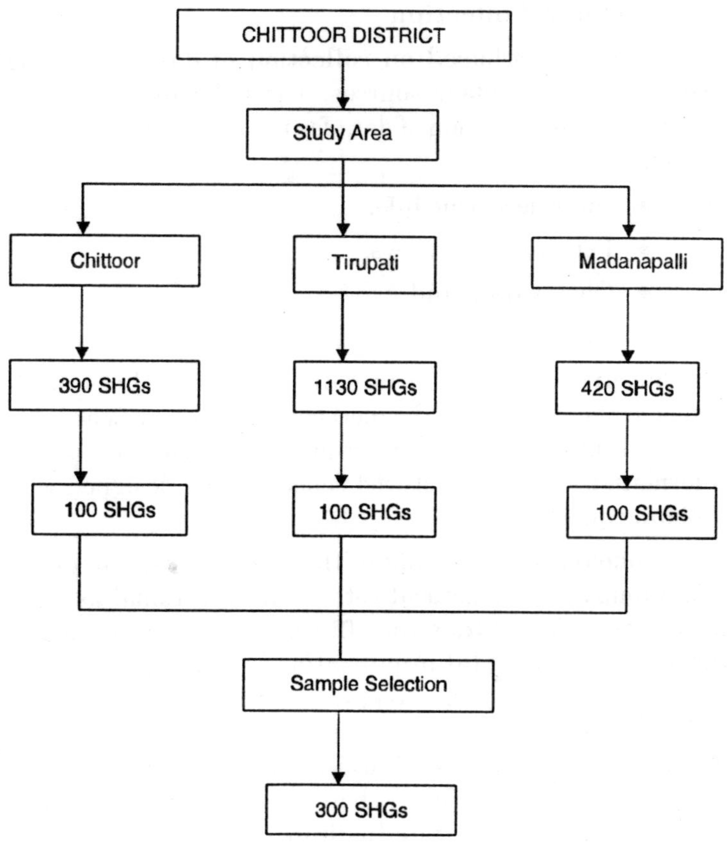

Fig.—3.1

Schematic Research Design of Sample Selection

Tools of Data Collection

The study is based on collection of data from both primary and secondary sources. The following tools were adopted for the collection of data for the present study. These include :

- Interview Schedule,
- Personal Interviews,
- Observation and
- Official Documents.

The primary data was collected from the sample respondents by adopting the methods of Interview Schedules, Personal Interviews and Observation. To elicit the required information, a well structured schedule was designed with probbing questions.

Secondary data relating to the different aspects of self help groups (the structural set up and functional aspects) have been collected from the official records maintained by the non governmental organisations in the district. The information regarding various activities of SHGs were collected from the offices of District Rural Development Agency (DRDA), Chief Planning Office (CPO), District Collectorate Office (DCO), National Institute of Rural Development (NIRD), State Institute of Rural Development (SIRD) and other Rural Banks, Co-operatives, Department of Women and Child Welfare, Women's Studies Centre, University libraries etc. The studies and reports brought out by the district rural development agencies of various districts and other published reports, Books, Articles in Journals, Newspaper clippings and district gazetteers were also referred to draw secondary data.

Analysis of Data

The collected data was analysed and tabulated. The data was scrutinized, verified and analysed with the help of computers. Frequency and percentages are computed for interpretation of the data. Apart from tabulation and analysis, necessary Graphs, Diagrams, are also incorporated in the study.

Chapter Scheme

The entire study is divided into five chapters and a brief description of each chapter is presented below.

In the first Chapter which is Introductory, the Concept of Empowerment and its Significance, Empowerment Approach to Development of Women, Origin of SHGs and self help groups Movement to Empower Women has been highlighted.

The second chapter consists of Review of relevant literature.

The third chapter deals with Research methodology such as Need and Importance of the study, Objectives, Sampling Design, Tools of data collection and finally Analysis of data.

The fourth Chapter is concerned with the results and discussions of the study.

The fifth Chapter brings out the Summary, Conclusions and Suggestions to strengthen the Self Help Groups.

4

RESULTS AND DISCUSSION

The study has been conducted in twelve Mandals (at the rate of four mandals from each revenue division). They are :

Tirupati Revenue Division

- Renigunta
- Srikalahasthi
- Pakala
- Varadaiah Palem

Chittoor Revenue Division

- Chittoor
- Vadamalpet
- Narayanavanam
- Irala

Madanapalli Revenue Division

- Chinnagottigallu
- Madanapalli
- K. V. Palli
- Kuppam

With in the study area again five panchayats from each mandal and five villages from each panchayat have been selected. A total sample of 300 beneficiaries had been selected for the study.

Table—4.1 Distribution of the respondents according to their age groups

Age	*TRD*				*CRD*				*MRD*				*Total*	*Percentage (%)*
	RGM	*SKM*	*PKM*	*VPM*	*CTM*	*VDM*	*NVM*	*IRM*	*CGM*	*MPM*	*KVM*	*KPM*		
<20	1	—	—	—	—	1	—	—	—	1	—	—	3	1.00
20-30	11	8	5	7	11	8	5	9	9	13	6	3	95	31.67
30-40	8	11	12	13	8	11	13	8	10	6	11	12	123	41.00
40-50	3	3	6	3	3	3	5	4	5	5	5	9	54	18.00
50-60	1	3	2	2	3	2	2	4	1	—	3	1	24	8.00
60>	1	—	—	—	—	—	—	—	—	—	—	—	1	0.33
Total	**25**	**25**	**25**	**25**	**25**	**25**	**25**	**25**	**25**	**25**	**25**	**25**	**300**	**100.00**

TRD : Tirupati Revenue Division
1.1 RGM : Renigunta Mandal
1.2 SKM : Srikalahasthi Mandal
1.3 PKM : Pakala Mandal
1.4 VPM : Varadaiahpalem Mandal

CRD : Chittoor Revenue Division
2.1 CTM : Chittoor Mandal
2.2 VDM : Vadamalpet Mandal
2.3 NVM : Narayana Vanam Mandal
2.4 IRM : Irala Mandal

MRD : Madanpalli Revenue Division
3.1 CGM : Chinnagottigallu Mandal
3.2 MPM : Madanpalli Mandal
3.3 KVM : K. V. Palli Mandal
3.4 KPM : Kuppam Mandal

The distribution of the respondents according to their age has been presented in Table-4.1. The data reveals that there are three respondents (1 per cent) below the age group of 20 years in RGM, VDM, MPM and only one respondent (0.33 per cent) in the age group of 60 years in RGM, 123 respondents (41 per cent) are in the age group of 30-40 years followed by 95 respondents (31.67 per cent) in the age group of 20-30 years.

It can be observed from the above table that most of the SHGs women (41 per cent) are in the age group of 30-40. The response among young women below 20 years is only 1 per cent. Here it highlights the need of motivating young women towards formation of SHGs.

Hinduism being the predominant Religion in India, it is not surprising to note that majority (96 per cent) of the respondents are Hindus. Only a small per cent (3.67 per cent) of Muslims and 0.33 per cent Christians are found as respondents in the study.

The status and life style of the respondents vary from caste to caste and also with in the caste, determined by the traditional occupation, work participation and social interaction patterns etc. It has been observed from Table-4.3 that about half of the respondents (50 per cent) belong to the backward caste category followed by scheduled caste category with 25.33 per cent, 20.67 per cent of the respondents belongs to OC and only four per cent are ST's.

Table-4.4 shows the nature of family of sample SHGs women. It is evident from table-4 that a large number 184 respondents (61.33 per cent) are living in nuclear families followed by 110 respondents (36.67 per cent) living in joint families, three respondents (one per cent) living in extended families and three respondents (one per cent) are living in single parent families. It shows that the traditional joint families are fast declining and nuclear families are on the rise even in rural areas. This is the impact of social transformation that is taking place in the society.

Table—4.2. Distribution of the respondents according to their religion

Caste	*TRD*				*CRD*				*MRD*				*Total*	*Percentage (%)*
	RGM	*SKM*	*PKM*	*VPM*	*CTM*	*VDM*	*NVM*	*IRM*	*CGM*	*MPM*	*KVM*	*KPM*		
Hindu	25	25	23	25	25	25	25	25	17	23	25	25	288	96.00
Muslim	—	—	2	—	—	—	—	—	8	1	—	—	11	3.67
Christian	—	—	—	—	—	—	—	—	—	1	—	—	1	0.33
Total	**25**	**25**	**25**	**25**	**25**	**25**	**25**	**25**	**25**	**25**	**25**	**25**	**300**	**100.00**

Table—4.3. Distribution of the respondents according to their caste

Caste	*TRD*				*CRD*				*MRD*				*Total*	*Percentage (%)*
	RGM	*SKM*	*PKM*	*VPM*	*CTM*	*VDM*	*NVM*	*IRM*	*CGM*	*MPM*	*KVM*	*KPM*		
OC	1	6	13	4	11	2	3	12	4	2	2	2	62	20.67
BC	17	12	5	3	7	16	22	8	16	18	11	15	150	50.00
SC	5	7	7	17	3	5	—	3	5	5	11	8	76	25.33
ST	2	—	—	1	4	2	—	2	—	—	1	—	12	4.00
Total	**25**	**25**	**25**	**25**	**25**	**25**	**25**	**25**	**25**	**25**	**25**	**25**	**300**	**100.00**

Table—4.4. Distribution of the respondents according to the nature of family

Nature of family	*TRD*				*CRD*				*MRD*				*Total*	*Percen-tage (%)*
	RGM	*SKM*	*PKM*	*VPM*	*CTM*	*VDM*	*NVM*	*IRM*	*CGM*	*MPM*	*KVM*	*KPM*		
Nuclear family	15	15	12	18	12	14	17	12	13	18	16	22	184	61.33
Joint family	8	10	13	7	13	9	8	12	12	7	8	3	110	36.67
Extended family	1	—	—	—	—	1	—	1	—	—	—	—	3	1.00
Single parent family	1	—	—	—	—	1	—	—	—	—	1	—	3	1.00
Total	25	25	25	25	25	25	25	25	25	25	25	25	300	100.00

Education is another factor which influences the status of SHG women. Education serves as a means towards change and development. It also helps to develop and create awareness about the ways of life through the acquisition of appropriate skills. It helps the individuals to overcome their prejudice and to support their family income. According to the data, (Table 4.5) 17.67 per cent of the respondents are illiterates, 9.33 per cent are literates, 10 per cent have lower primary education, 12.33 per cent have primary, 25.33 per cent have upper primary, 17.67 per cent have high school education, 6.67 per cent have college education and only one per cent of the respondents have technical education. In all the three mandals the number of upper primary education and those who possessed high school education is high.

Table-4.6 shows distribution of the respondents according to their age and education. The above table reveals that out of 300 sample respondents, 8 respondents are in the age group of less than 20, 124 respondents are in the age group of 20-30, 114 respondents are in the age group of 30-40, 48 respondents are in the age group of 40-50, five respondents are in the age group of 50-60 and only one respondent is in the age group of 60 and above.

Among 53 illiterates, 19 respondents are in the age group of 20-30, 20 respondents are in the age group of 30-40, 13 respondents are in the age group of 40-50, and only one respondent is in the age group of 50-60. Among 28 literates 12 respondents are in the age group of 20-30, 9 respondents are in the age group of 30-40, five respondents are in the age group of 40-50, one respondent is in the age group of 50-60 and one respondent is in the above 60 years age group. Among lower primary *i.e.* 30 respondents two respondents are in the age group less than 20, 11 respondents are in the age group of 20-30, 10 respondents are in the age group of 30-40, 6 respondents are in the age group of 40-50 and only one respondent is in the age group of 50-60. Among 37 respondents have primary education. Out of 37, eight respondents are in the age group of 20-30, 21 respondents are in the age group of 30-40, 7 respondents are in the age group of 40-50 and only one respondent is in the age group of 50-60. According to the table, 76 respondents are having upper primary education. Out of 76 respondents 4 respondents are in the age group of less than 20, 29 respondents are in the age group of 20-30, 30 respondents are in the age group of 30-40, 12 respondents are in the age group of 40-50, and only one respondent is in the age group of 50-60. Followed by 53 respondents are having high school education. Out of 53 respondents, one respondent is in the age group of less than 20. 33 respondents are in the age group of 20-30, 14 respondents are in the age group of 30-40 and five respondents are in the age group of 40-50. 18 respondents are having intermediate. Out of 18 one respondent is in the age group of less than 20,10 respondents are in the age group of 20-30 and seven respondents are in the age group of 30-40. Three respondents are having technical education. Out of three one respondent is in the age group of 20-30 and two respondents are in the age group of 30-40. Two respondents are having Degree qualification. Out of two, one respondent is in the age group of 20-30 and one respondent is in the age group of 30-40.

Table-4.7 reveals that out of 300 respondents, 18 OC respondents have primary education, 28 OC respondents have upper primary education and 12 OC respondents have high school education. Among BCs 24 respondents are illiterates, 23 BC respondents are literates, 34 BC respondents are having upper primary and 22 BC respondents are having high school education. Among SCs 22 respondents are illiterates, 12 SC respondents are having upper primary and 18 SC respondents are having high school education. Among STs four respondents are illiterates, three ST respondents have lower primary and two ST respondents have upper primary education.

Table-4.8 shows the Marital status of the respondents. According to the data, higher percentage (89 per cent) of the respondents are married, 9 per cent of the respondents are widowed and one per cent of the respondents are unmarried and one per cent are separated. The above table shows that one per cent of the unmarried women are also joined in Self Help Groups.

Table—4.5. Distribution of the respondents according to their educational levels

Educational level	*TRD*				*CRD*				*MRD*				*Total*	*Percentage (%)*
	RGM	*SKM*	*PKM*	*VPM*	*CTM*	*VDM*	*NVM*	*IRM*	*CGM*	*MPM*	*KVM*	*KPM*		
Illiterate	2	1	2	6	6	1	3	4	3	3	11	11	53	17.67
Literate	6	1	—	2	2	6	—	3	1	1	2	4	28	9.33
Lower primary	2	1	1	7	3	2	3	3	3	2	1	2	30	10.00
Primary	5	4	3	4	1	3	5	1	3	6	—	2	37	12.33
Upper primary	4	10	7	2	11	6	7	12	8	3	3	3	76	25.33
High school	5	7	7	2	2	6	2	2	4	9	5	2	53	17.67
Intermediate	1	1	3	1	—	1	4	—	3	1	3	—	18	6.00
Technical education	—	—	2	—	—	—	1	—	—	—	—	—	3	1.00
Degree	—	—	—	1	—	—	—	—	—	—	—	1	2	0.67
Total	**25**	**25**	**25**	**25**	**25**	**25**	**25**	**25**	**25**	**25**	**25**	**25**	**300**	**100.00**

Table—4.6. Distribution of the respondents according to their age and education

Age Group (in Years)	*Tirupati*										*Chittoor*									
	1	*2*	*3*	*4*	*5*	*6*	*7*	*8*	*9*	*Total*	*1*	*2*	*3*	*4*	*5*	*6*	*7*	*8*	*9*	*Total*
<20	—	—	1	—	1	—	—	—	—	2	1	—	1	—	2	—	—	—	—	3
20-30	4	4	3	5	8	13	4	1	1	43	4	6	4	2	15	6	2	—	—	39
30-40	4	3	5	7	10	5	2	1	—	37	5	4	3	7	13	5	3	1	—	41
40-50	3	1	1	3	3	3	—	—	—	14	4	—	3	1	6	1	—	—	—	15
50-60	—	—	1	1	1	—	—	—	—	3	1	1	1	—	—	—	—	—	—	2
60>	—	1	—	—	—	—	—	—	—	1	—	—	—	—	—	—	—	—	—	—
Total	11	9	11	16	23	21	6	2	1	100	14	11	11	10	36	12	5	1	—	100

Age Group (in Years)	*Madanapalle*										*Grand total*									
	1	*2*	*3*	*4*	*5*	*6*	*7*	*8*	*9*	*Total*	*1*	*2*	*3*	*4*	*5*	*6*	*7*	*8*	*9*	*Total*
<20	—	—	—	—	1	1	1	—	—	3	—	—	2	—	4	1	1	—	—	8
20-30	11	2	4	1	6	14	4	—	—	42	19	12	11	8	29	33	10	1	1	124
30-40	11	2	2	7	7	4	2	—	1	36	20	9	10	21	30	14	7	2	1	114
40-50	6	4	2	3	3	1	—	—	—	19	13	5	6	7	1	5	—	—	—	48
50-60	—	—	—	—	—	—	—	—	—	—	1	1	1	1	1	—	—	—	—	5
60>	—	—	—	—	—	—	—	—	—	—	—	1	—	—	—	—	—	—	—	1
Total	28	8	8	11	17	20	7	—	1	100	53	28	30	37	76	53	18	3	2	300

Note : 1. Illiterate, 2. Literate, 3. Lower Primary, 4. Primary, 5. Upper Primary, 6. High School, 7. Intermediate, 8. Technical Education, 9. Degree.

Table—4.7. Education and caste wise distribution of the respondents

Education	Tirupati					Chittoor					Madanapalli					Grand Total				
	OC	BC	SC	ST	Total	OC	BC	SC	ST	Total	OC	BC	SC	ST	Total	OC	BC	SC	ST	Total
Illiterate	2	3	7	—	12	2	5	3	4	14	—	16	12	—	28	4	24	22	4	54
Literate	—	7	2	—	9	—	9	2	—	11	—	7	1	—	8	—	23	5	—	28
Lower primary	2	2	5	2	11	3	7	—	1	11	1	7	—	—	8	6	16	5	3	30
Primary	6	6	3	—	15	2	6	1	1	10	10	—	1	—	11	18	12	5	1	36
Upper primary	6	11	6	—	23	14	16	4	2	36	8	7	2	—	17	28	34	12	2	76
High school	5	6	10	—	21	6	6	—	—	12	1	10	8	1	20	12	22	18	1	53
Intermediate	2	2	2	—	6	1	3	1	—	5	1	1	5	—	7	4	6	8	—	18
Technical education	2	—	—	—	2	—	1	—	—	1	—	—	—	—	—	2	1	—	—	3
Degree	—	—	1	—	1	—	—	—	—	—	1	—	—	—	1	1	—	1	—	2
Total	**25**	**37**	**36**	**2**	**100**	**28**	**53**	**11**	**8**	**100**	**22**	**48**	**29**	**1**	**100**	**75**	**138**	**76**	**11**	**300**

Table—4.8. Distribution of the respondents according to their marital status

Marital status	*TRD*				*CRD*				*MRD*				*Total*	*Percen-tage (%)*
	RGM	*SKM*	*PKM*	*VPM*	*CTM*	*VDM*	*NVM*	*IRM*	*CGM*	*MPM*	*KVM*	*KPM*		
Married	21	23	18	24	24	22	20	24	23	23	23	22	267	89.00
Unmarried	1	—	—	—	—	—	1	—	1	—	—	—	3	1.00
Separated	—	—	—	—	—	—	2	—	—	—	—	1	3	1.00
Widowed	3	2	7	1	1	3	2	1	1	2	2	2	27	9.00
Divorced	—	—	—	—	—	—	—	—	—	—	—	—	—	—
Total	**25**	**25**	**25**	**25**	**25**	**25**	**25**	**25**	**25**	**25**	**25**	**25**	**300**	**100.00**

Table—4.9. Distribution of the respondents according to their age at marriage

Age at Marriage	*TRD*				*CRD*				*MRD*				*Total*	*Percentage (%)*
	RGM	*SKM*	*PKM*	*VPM*	*CTM*	*VDM*	*NVM*	*IRM*	*CGM*	*MPM*	*KVM*	*KPM*		
< 14 years	8	2	1	14	9	8	3	9	1	8	7	4	74	24.67
15-20	14	20	19	9	16	14	18	16	21	16	16	19	198	66.00
20-25	2	3	4	1	—	3	3	—	2	1	2	1	22	7.30
25-30	—	—	1	1	—	—	—	—	—	—	—	1	3	1.00
Not applicable	1	—	—	—	—	—	1	—	1	—	—	—	3	1.00
Total	**25**	**25**	**25**	**25**	**25**	**25**	**25**	**25**	**25**	**25**	**25**	**25**	**300**	**100.00**

Table-4.9 shows age at marriage of the respondents. According to the data, 198 respondents (66 per cent) are married in the age group of 15-20 years followed by 74 respondents (24.67 per cent) married before 14 years of age, 22 respondents (7.30 per cent) are married in the age group of 20-25 years and three respondents (1 per cent) are married in the age group of 25-30 years. The data reveals that even now child marriages are taking place in rural areas.

Diverse occupations are observed among the respondents in Table-4.10. The data in this table shows that the majority of the respondents are working as coolies. 50 respondents (16.67 per cent) have dairying followed by 41 respondents (31.67 per cent) have cultivation, 31 respondents (10.33 per cent) have business, 24 respondents (8 per cent) are house wives, 22 respondents (7.33 per cent) are tailors, 17 respondents (5.67 per cent) have private jobs and only three respondents (one per cent) main occupation is carpentry.

Table-4.11 gives a picture of distribution of respondents according to their main occupation and caste. The table shows that 110 respondents are working as coolies, followed by 42 respondents have cultivation, 50 respondents have dairying, 32 respondents have business, 22 respondents have tailoring and three respondents have the occupation of carpentry. Only 17 respondents have private jobs.

According to the table, among 70 OC respondents 17 respondents are working as coolies, 11 respondents are engaged in cultivation and 23 respondents have dairying. Among 143 BCs, 47 respondents are working as coolies, 25 respondents have dairying and 23 respondents have business. Among 75 SCs, 37 respondents are working as coolies, 13 respondents have cultivation and 7 respondents have tailoring. Among 12 STs, 9 respondents are working as coolies, two respondents are house wives and only one respondent is engaged in tailoring.

Table-4.12 gives detailed information of the respondents main occupation and education.

Table-4.12 clearly shows the relation between education and selection of main occupation. It is interesting to note that majority of the respondents *i.e.,* 112 out of 300 irrespective of their educational status engaged as coolies. Out of 112 respondents, 37 respondents are illiterates, 21 respondents are having upper primary, 16 respondents are having lower primary education. Followed by 51 respondents out of 300, irrespective of their educational status are engaged in dairying. Out of 51 respondents, 22 respondents are having upper primary education, 12 respondents are having primary education and only seven respondents have high school education. Among 41 respondents irrespective of their educational status are engaged in cultivation. Out of 41 respondents, 11 respondents have high school education, nine respondents have primary and seven have upper primary education. This reveals that SHGs still needs some more campaigning and motivation to become educated.

Table-4.13 shows distribution of the respondents according to their income per month. According to the data, 120 respondents (40 per cent) family income ranged from Rs. 1000-2000 followed by 75 respondents (25 per cent) family income ranged from Rs. 2000-3000. 50 respondents (16.67 per cent) family income is below Rs. 1000 and 35 respondents (11.67 per cent) family income ranged from Rs. 3000-4000. The rest of them are earning more than Rs. 5000 per month.

The data in Table-4.14 shows authority of the respondents on their earnings. According to the data, 188 respondents (62.67 per cent) told that both wife and husband have the authority on earnings, 78 respondents (26 per cent) have the authority to use their earnings and 20 respondents (6.67 per cent) told that all members of the family have the authority on the earnings of the respondents. The rest of them told that their parents and husbands have the authority to use their earnings.

The above table represents that the expenditure of the 103 respondents (34.33 per cent) is Rs. 20,000-30,000, 94 respondents (31.33 per cent) is Rs. 10,000-20,000, 47 respondents (15.67 per cent) is Rs. 30,000-40,000, 28 respondents (9.33 per cent) is below Rs. 10,000, 17 respondents (5.67 per cent) is Rs. 40,000-50,000 and six respondents (2 per cent) is Rs. 50,000-60,000. Only the small number *i.e.* five respondents (1.67 per cent) house hold expenditure per annum is above Rs. 60,000/-.

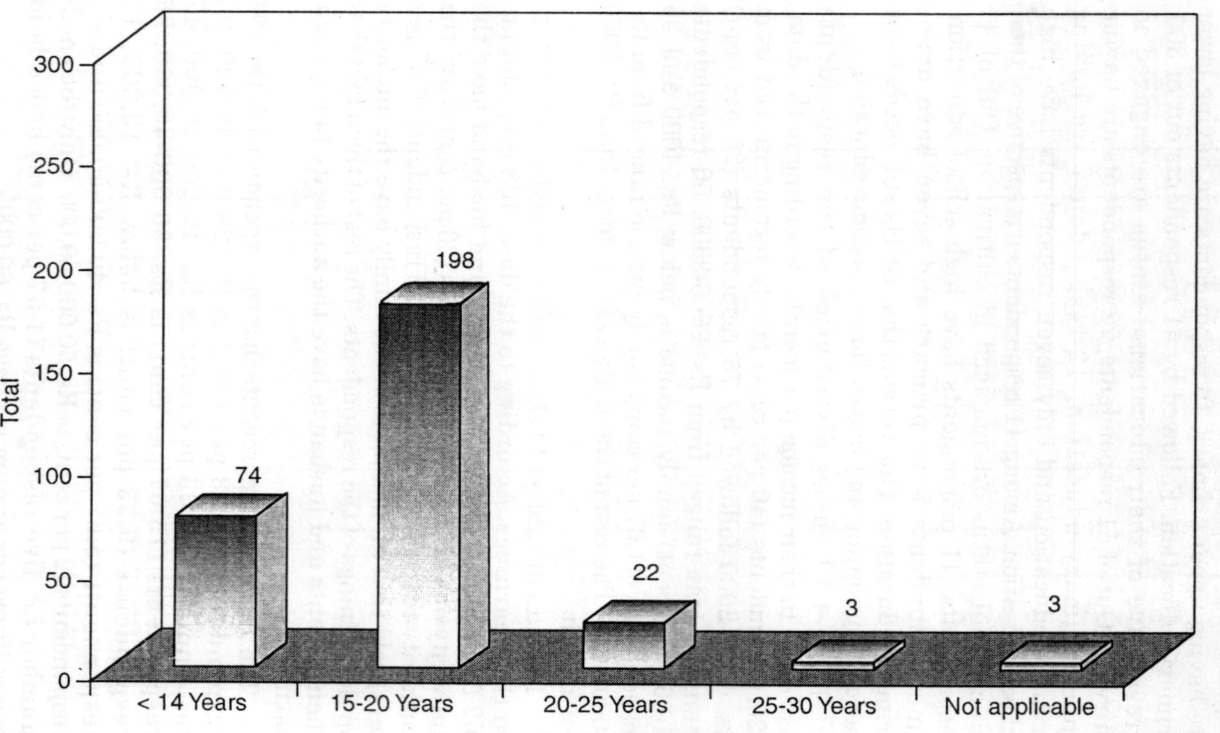

Fig. 1. Distribution of the respondents according to their age at marriage

Table—4.10. Distribution of the respondents according to their main occupation

Occupation	*TRD*				*CRD*				*MRD*				*Total*	*Percentage (%)*
	RGM	*SKM*	*PKM*	*VPM*	*CTM*	*VDM*	*NVM*	*IRM*	*CGM*	*MPM*	*KVM*	*KPM*		
Cooly	7	11	8	16	11	7	6	11	7	4	17	7	112	37.33
Cultivation	5	7	4	5	1	7	4	2	3	2	1	—	41	13.67
Dairying	3	6	2	2	7	4	10	4	3	5	2	2	50	16.67
Business	3	—	2	—	1	3	1	2	6	3	—	10	31	10.33
Private job	2	1	3	1	—	—	2	1	1	4	—	2	17	5.67
Tailoring	4	—	4	1	1	4	1	2	—	3	2	—	22	7.33
House wife	1	—	2	—	4	—	1	3	5	1	3	4	24	8.00
Carpentry	—	—	—	—	—	—	—	—	—	3	—	—	3	1.00
Total	**25**	**25**	**25**	**25**	**25**	**25**	**25**	**25**	**25**	**25**	**25**	**25**	**300**	**100.00**

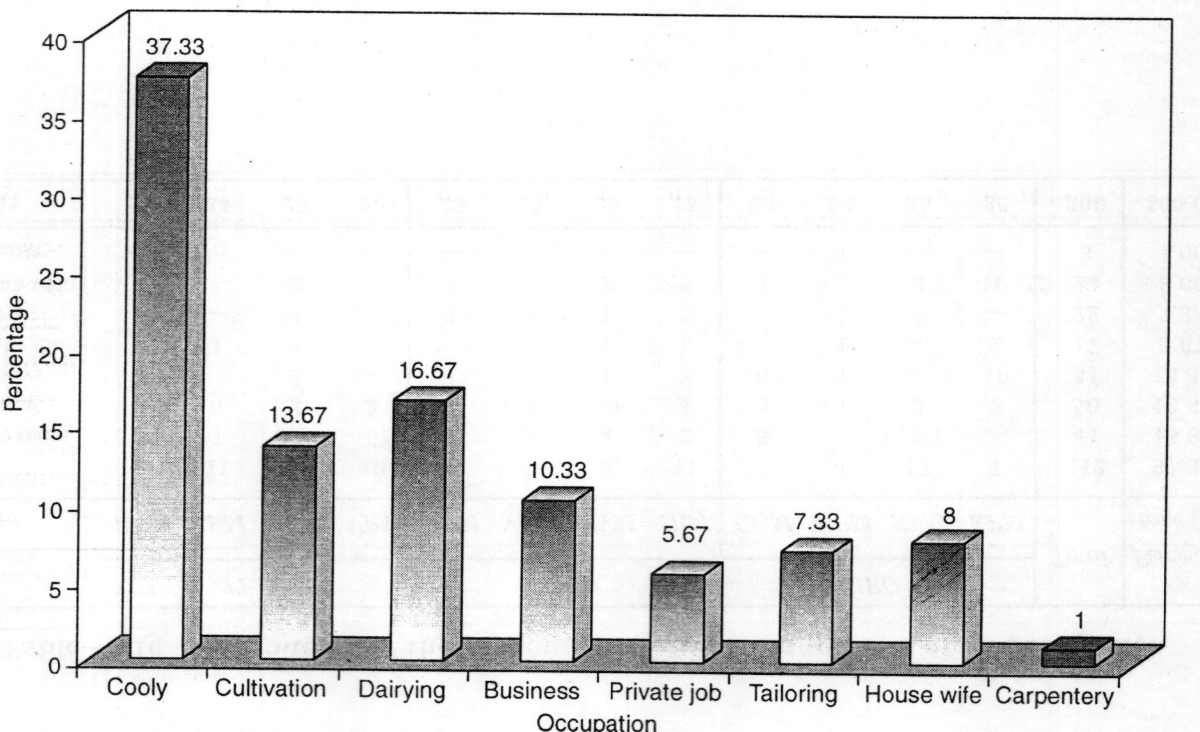

Fig. 2. Distribution of the respondents according to their main occupation

Table—4.11. Occupation and caste wise distribution of the respondents

Occupation	*Tirupati*					*Chittoor*					*Madanapalli*					*Grand Total*				
	OC	*BC*	*SC*	*ST*	*Total*	*OC*	*BC*	*SC*	*ST*	*Total*	*OC*	*BC*	*SC*	*ST*	*Total*	*OC*	*BC*	*SC*	*ST*	*Total*
Cooly	4	14	21	3	42	10	16	2	6	34	3	17	14	—	34	17	47	37	9	110
Cultivation	7	7	7	—	21	4	7	3	—	14	—	4	3	—	7	11	18	13	—	42
Dairying	7	5	1	—	13	14	11	—	—	25	2	9	1	—	12	23	25	2	—	50
Business	—	5	—	—	5	5	2	1	—	8	—	16	3	—	19	5	23	4	—	32
Private job	2	2	3	—	7	—	3	—	—	3	1	4	2	—	7	3	9	5	—	17
Tailoring	2	3	4	—	9	2	4	2	—	8	—	3	1	1	5	4	10	7	1	22
House wife	2	1	—	—	3	1	3	2	2	8	3	6	4	—	13	6	10	6	2	24
Carpentry	—	—	—	—	—	—	—	—	—	—	1	1	1	—	3	1	1	1	—	3
Total	**24**	**37**	**36**	**3**	**100**	**36**	**46**	**10**	**8**	**100**	**10**	**60**	**29**	**1**	**100**	**70**	**143**	**75**	**12**	**300**

Table—4.12. Distribution of the respondents according to their main occupation and education

Main Occupation	*Tirupati*										*Chittoor*									
	1	*2*	*3*	*4*	*5*	*6*	*7*	*8*	*9*	*Total*	*1*	*2*	*3*	*4*	*5*	*6*	*7*	*8*	*9*	*Total*
Cooly	8	4	8	4	9	8	1	—	—	42	12	5	4	3	7	4	—	—	—	35
Cultivation	1	—	2	5	6	5	2	—	—	21	—	1	2	3	1	4	3	—	—	14
Dairying	—	1	1	4	4	2	1	—	—	13	1	—	2	4	15	3	—	—	—	25
Business	—	2	—	1	1	1	—	—	—	5	—	2	1	—	3	1	—	—	—	7
Private job	—	1	—	—	1	3	1	—	1	7	—	1	—	—	—	—	1	1	—	3
Tailoring	2	1	—	1	2	2	1	—	—	9	1	2	—	—	5	—	—	—	—	8
House wife	—	—	—	1	—	—	—	2	—	3	—	—	2	—	5	—	1	—	—	8
Carpentry	—	—	—	—	—	—	—	—	—	—	—	—	—	—	—	—	—	—	—	—
Total	**11**	**9**	**11**	**16**	**23**	**21**	**6**	**2**	**1**	**100**	**14**	**11**	**11**	**10**	**36**	**12**	**5**	**1**	**—**	**100**

(*Contd.*)

Table—4.12 (*Contd.*). Distribution of the respondents according to their main occupation and education

Main Occupation	Madanapalli										Grand Total									
	1	*2*	*3*	*4*	*5*	*6*	*7*	*8*	*9*	*Total*	*1*	*2*	*3*	*4*	*5*	*6*	*7*	*8*	*9*	*Total*
Cooly	17	3	4	1	5	3	2	—	—	35	37	12	16	8	21	15	3	—	—	112
Cultivation	2	—	—	1	—	2	1	—	—	6	3	1	4	9	7	11	6	—	—	41
Dairying	1	—	1	4	3	2	2	—	—	13	2	1	4	12	22	7	3	—	—	51
Business	5	5	—	4	4	1	—	—	—	19	5	9	1	5	8	3	—	—	—	31
Private job	—	—	—	—	—	5	1	—	—	6	—	2	—	—	1	8	3	1	1	16
Tailoring	1	—	1	—	1	2	—	—	—	5	4	3	1	1	8	4	1	—	—	22
House wife	1	—	2	1	5	4	—	—	—	13	1	—	4	2	10	4	1	2	—	24
Carpentry	1	—	—	—	—	1	1	—	—	3	1	—	—	—	—	1	1	—	—	3
Total	**28**	**8**	**8**	**11**	**18**	**20**	**7**	—	—	**100**	**53**	**28**	**30**	**37**	**77**	**53**	**18**	**3**	**1**	**300**

Note : 1. Illiterate, 2. Literate, 3. Lower primary, 4. Primary, 5. Upper Primary, 6. High School, 7. Intermediate, 8. Technical education, 9. Degree.

Table—4.13. Distribution of the respondents according to their income P/M (per month)

Income in Rs.	*TRD*				*CRD*				*MRD*				*Total*	*Percen-tage (%)*
	RGM	*SKM*	*PKM*	*VPM*	*CTM*	*VDM*	*NVM*	*IRM*	*CGM*	*MPM*	*KVM*	*KPM*		
<-1000	1	2	3	4	10	1	4	11	3	1	6	4	50	16.67
1000-2000	13	7	11	13	10	10	13	9	7	8	9	10	120	40.00
2000-3000	6	8	7	7	3	10	5	3	7	9	6	4	75	25.00
3000-4000	4	5	1	1	2	4	2	2	1	4	3	6	35	11.67
4000-5000	1	—	2	—	—	—	1	—	1	2	1	—	8	2.67
5000-6000	—	2	—	—	—	—	—	—	3	—	—	—	5	1.67
6000-7000	—	—	—	—	—	—	—	—	1	1	—	—	2	0.67
7000-8000	—	—	—	—	—	—	—	—	1	—	—	—	1	0.33
8000-9000	—	—	—	—	—	—	—	—	—	—	—	—	—	—
9000-10000	—	1	1	—	—	—	—	—	—	—	—	—	2	0.67
10000 & >	—	—	—	—	—	—	—	—	1	—	—	1	2	0.67
Total	**25**	**25**	**25**	**25**	**25**	**25**	**25**	**25**	**25**	**25**	**25**	**25**	**300**	**100.00**

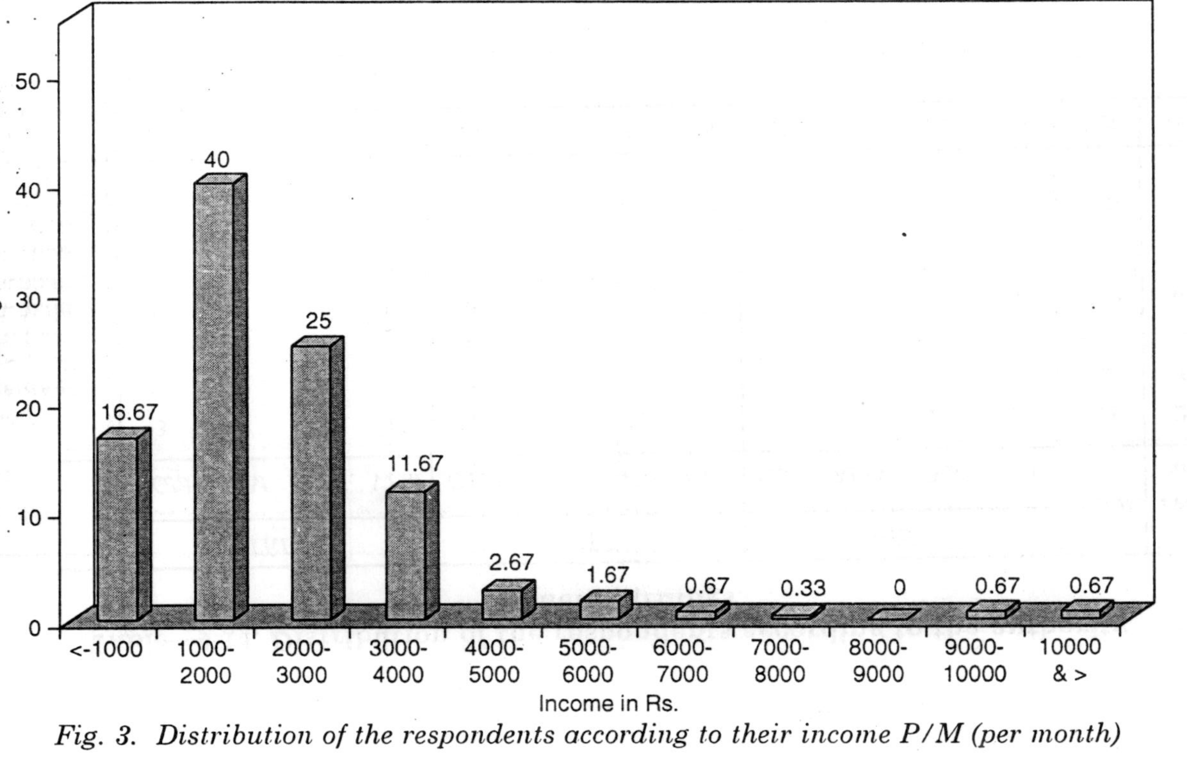

Fig. 3. Distribution of the respondents according to their income P/M (per month)

Table—4.14. Distribution of the respondents according to the authority on their earnings

Authority	*TRD*				*CRD*				*MRD*				*Total*	*Percen-tage (%)*
	RGM	*SKM*	*PKM*	*VPM*	*CTM*	*VDM*	*NVM*	*IRM*	*CGM*	*MPM*	*KVM*	*KPM*		
My self	3	4	12	6	7	3	10	8	3	4	12	6	78	26.00
Parents	—	—	—	—	1	—	—	1	—	—	—	—	2	0.67
Husband	—	—	—	—	6	—	—	6	—	—	—	—	12	4.00
Both Wife & Husband	20	20	11	19	8	19	13	8	20	20	11	19	188	62.67
Any other (Specify)/All members	2	1	2	—	3	3	2	2	2	1	2	—	20	6.67
Total	**25**	**25**	**25**	**25**	**25**	**25**	**25**	**25**	**25**	**25**	**25**	**25**	**300**	**100.00**

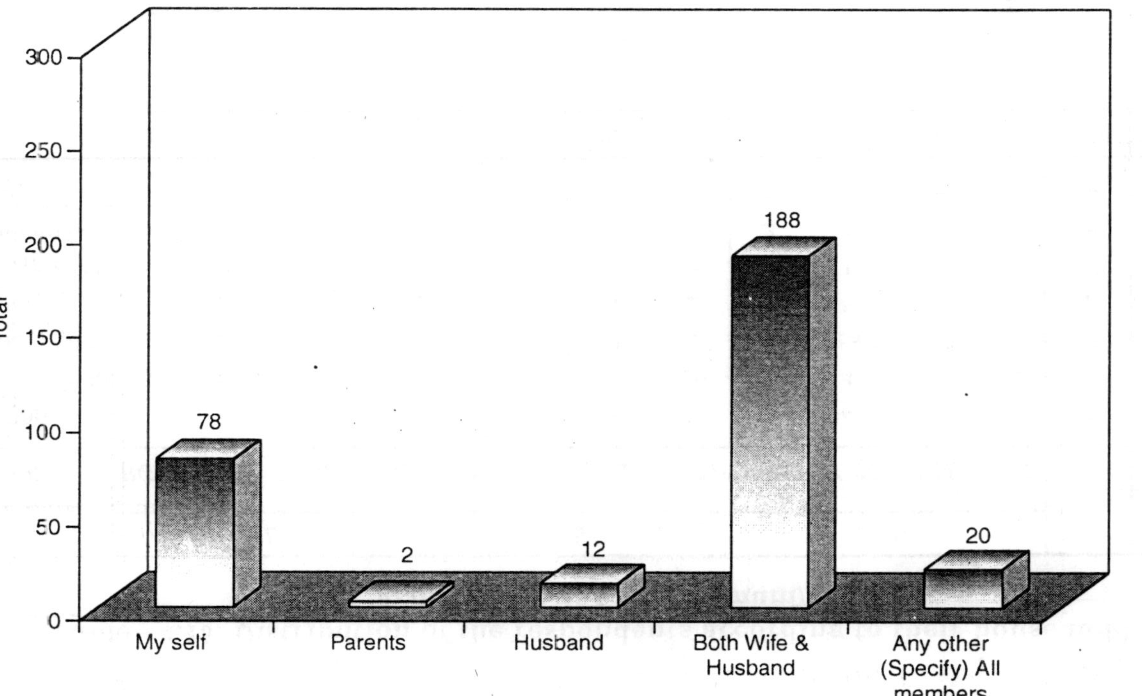

Fig. 4. Distribution of the respondents according to the authority on their earnings.

Table—4.15. Distribution of the respondents according to their house hold expenditure P/A (Per Annum)

Expenditure	*TRD*				*CRD*				*MRD*				*Total*	*Percen-*
P/A in Rs.	*RGM*	*SKM*	*PKM*	*VPM*	*CTM*	*VDM*	*NVM*	*IRM*	*CGM*	*MPM*	*KVM*	*KPM*		*tage (%)*
<-10,000	—	—	2	1	6	—	1	7	4	—	5	2	28	9.33
10,000-20,000	8	8	7	13	11	7	7	10	2	4	9	8	94	31.33
20,000-30,000	8	12	14	6	3	9	9	4	9	13	8	8	103	34.33
30,000-40,000	8	2	1	4	3	8	4	2	2	5	3	5	47	15.67
40,000-50,000	1	2	1	—	2	1	4	2	2	1	—	1	17	5.67
50,000-60,000	—	1	—	1	—	—	—	—	2	1	—	1	6	2.00
60,000 & >	—	—	—	—	—	—	—	—	4	1	—	—	5	1.67
Total	**25**	**25**	**25**	**25**	**25**	**25**	**25**	**25**	**25**	**25**	**25**	**25**	**300**	**100.00**

Table—4.16. Distribution of the respondents according to decision making

Decision Making	*TRD*				*CRD*				*MRD*				*Total*	*Percentage (%)*
	RGM	*SKM*	*PKM*	*VPM*	*CTM*	*VDM*	*NVM*	*IRM*	*CGM*	*MPM*	*KVM*	*KPM*		
Yes	25	23	25	24	24	24	25	24	24	25	25	24	292	97.33
No	—	2	—	1	1	1	—	1	1	—	—	1	8	2.67
Total	**25**	**25**	**25**	**25**	**25**	**25**	**25**	**25**	**25**	**25**	**25**	**25**	**300**	**100.00**

Table-4.16 shows distribution of the respondents according to the decision making. According to the data, 292 respondents (97.33 per cent) have the power to take decisions in important issues and only 8 respondents (2.67 per cent) have no decision making power. This shows that the higher percentage of women have the decision making power on important issues.

Table-4.17 shows the decision making of the respondents in the family. According to the data, regarding movable and immovable property 15.33 per cent of the respondents have the decision making power and only 5.67 per cent of all members of the family including the respondent have the decision making power.

According to the data, regarding savings 18 per cent of the respondents have decision making power and 5.67 per cent of all members of the family including the respondent have the decision making power.

Regarding expenditure 15.67 per cent of the respondents have the decision making power and 5.67 per cent of all members of the family including respondents have the decision making power.

Regarding house hold articles 15.67 per cent of the respondents, regarding children's education 15.33 per cent, children's marriage 15 per cent, regarding family planning 16.67 per cent and with regard to where to live and how to live 16.67 per cent of the respondents have the decision making power.

Table-4.18 & 4.18A represents the details of information related to assets of the respondents. According to the table, 91.67 per cent have the assets. Diverse assets are observed among the beneficiaries. Assets are two types. They are movable and immovable assets. Higher percentage of the respondents have the immovable assets and 63.33 per cent have the movable assets.

Table-4.19 shows distribution of the respondents according to the amount of over all savings. According to the data, 8 respondents (26.67 per cent) have over all savings ranged from Rs. 20,000-30,000 followed by 55 respondents (18.33 per cent) have over all savings ranged from Rs. 30,000-40,000, 47 respondents (15.67 per cent) have over all savings ranged from Rs. 10,000-20,000 and 42 respondents (14 per cent) have over all savings below Rs. 10,000. The rest of the respondents have over all savings of above Rs. 50,000/-.

Table-4.20 shows distribution of the respondents according to their savings. According to the data, 296 respondents (98.67 per cent) are saving money monthly and only 4 respondents (1.33 per cent) are saving money weekly.

Table-4.21 shows distribution of the respondents according to their amount of savings per month. According to the data, only 0.33 percent are saving the money from Rs. 40-50/-. But above half of the respondents are saving the money from Rs. 30-40/- and 139 respondents (46.33 per cent) are saving the money above Rs. 50/- per month.

Table-4.22 shows distribution of the respondents according to the maintenance of records of their savings. According to the data, 100 per cent of the respondents are maintaining records very perfectly for their savings.

Table-4.23 shows the distribution of the respondents according to their debts. According to the data, 271 respondents (90.33 per cent) have debts and 29 respondents (9.67 per cent) told that they have no debts.

Table-4.24 shows distribution of the respondents according to the source of debts. According to the data, 146 respondents (48.67 per cent) have taken loans from their group members, followed by 79 respondents (26.33 per cent) from banks, 29 respondents (9.67 per cent) from others and 28 respondents (9.33 per cent) from private individuals. The rest of the respondents have taken loans from money lenders, friends and hand loans.

Table-4.25 shows distribution of the respondents according to their repayment of debts. According to the data, 242 respondents (80.67 per cent) repay their debts by doing hard work, followed by 31 respondents (10.33 per cent) told that they do not know how to repay their debts, 14 respondents (4.67 per cent) repay their debts by instalments out of savings occured. The remaining respondents repay their debts from chit fund, by getting dowry for male child and by selling of house.

Table—4.17. Distribution of the respondents according to the decision making in the family

Decision Making		*Respondent*	*Respondent & Her Husband*	*Only Husband*	*Respondent Husband & Elder children*	*All members of the family excluding respondent*	*All members of the family including respondent*	*Only elder family members*	*Others*
1	*2*	*3*	*4*	*5*	*6*	*7*	*8*	*9*	*10*
Regarding	TRD	12	70	4	2	6	3	2	1
movable and	CRD	20	63	3	2	—	8	2	2
immovable	MRD	14	70	8	—	—	6	1	1
property	Total	46	203	15	4	6	17	5	4
	Percentage (%)	15.33	67.67	5.00	1.33	2.00	5.67	1.67	1.33
Regarding	TRD	13	72	1	1	7	3	2	1
savings	CRD	22	64	2	—	1	8	2	1
	MRD	19	69	5	—	—	6	—	1
	Total	54	205	8	1	8	17	4	3
	Percentage (%)	18.00	68.33	2.67	0.33	2.67	5.67	1.33	1

(Contd.)

1	2	3	4	5	6	7	8	9	10
Regarding	TRD	12	72	2	1	7	3	2	1
expenditure	CRD	20	64	2	1	1	8	2	2
	MRD	15	70	7	—	—	6	1	1
	Total	47	206	11	2	8	17	5	4
	Percentage (%)	15.67	68.67	3.67	0.67	2.67	5.67	1.67	1.33
Regarding	TRD	12	72	2	1	7	3	2	1
house hold	CRD	20	64	2	1	1	8	2	2
articles	MRD	15	71	6	—	—	6	1	1
	Total	47	207	10	2	8	17	5	4
	Percentage (%)	15.67	69.00	3.33	0.67	2.67	5.67	1.67	1.33
Regarding	TRD	12	73	1	1	7	3	2	1
childrens	CRD	20	65	1	1	1	8	2	2
education	MRD	14	71	6	1	—	6	1	1
	Total	46	209	8	3	8	17	5	4
	Percentage (%)	15.33	69.67	2.67	1.00	2.67	5.67	1.67	1.33

(Contd.)

1	2	3	4	5	6	7	8	9	10
Regarding	TRD	12	71	3	2	6	3	2	1
marriage	CRD	19	64	3	2	—	8	2	2
	MRD	14	70	7	—	—	7	1	1
	Total	45	205	13	4	6	18	5	4
	Percentage (%)	15.00	68.33	4.33	1.33	2.00	6.00	1.66	1.33
Regarding	TRD	13	73	1	1	6	3	2	1
family planning	CRD	23	63	1	1	—	8	2	2
	MRD	14	72	6	—	—	6	1	1
	Total	50	208	8	2	6	17	5	4
	Percentage (%)	16.67	69.33	2.67	0.67	2.00	5.67	1.67	1.33
Regarding	TRD	13	72	2	1	6	3	2	1
where to live	CRD	23	62	2	1	—	8	2	2
& how to	MRD	14	70	8	—	—	6	1	1
live	Total	50	204	12	2	6	17	5	4
	Percentage (%)	16.67	68	4.00	0.67	2.00	5.67	1.67	1.33

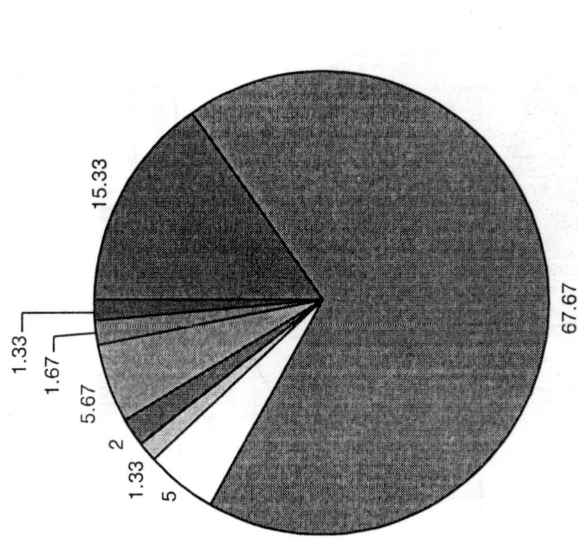

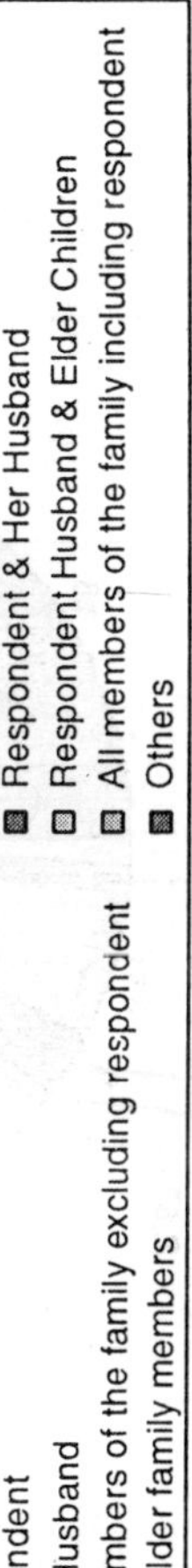

Fig. 5a Distribution of the respondents according to the decision making in the family

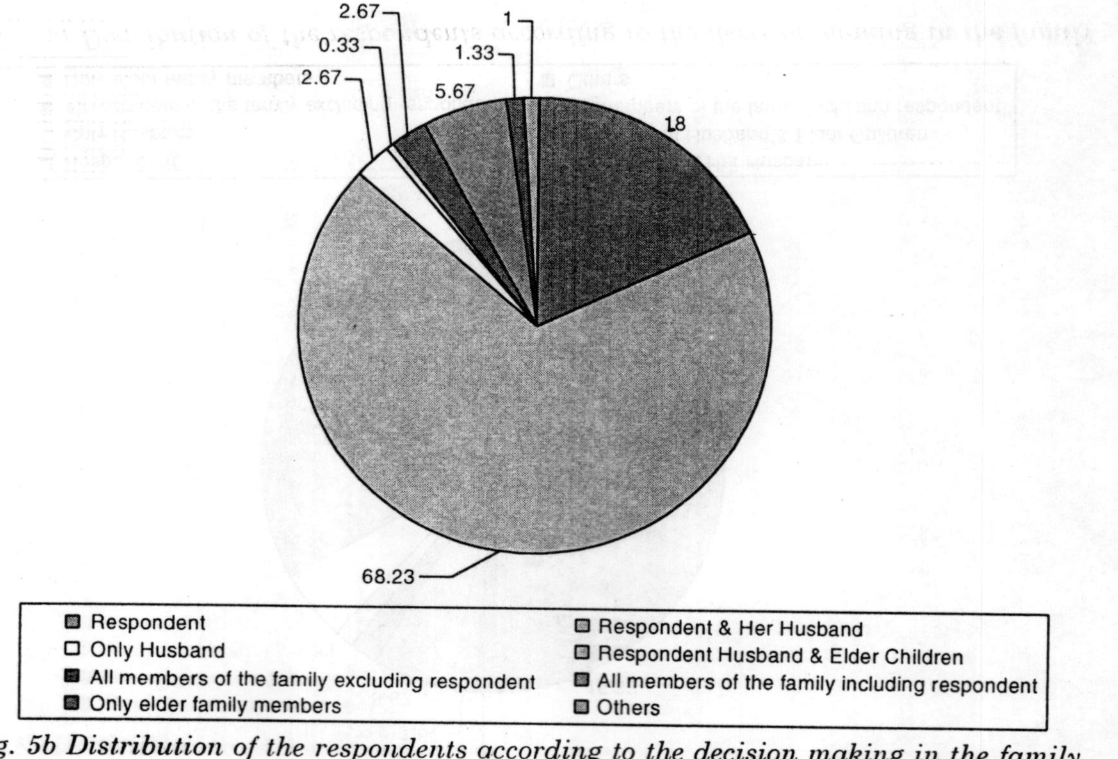

Fig. 5b Distribution of the respondents according to the decision making in the family

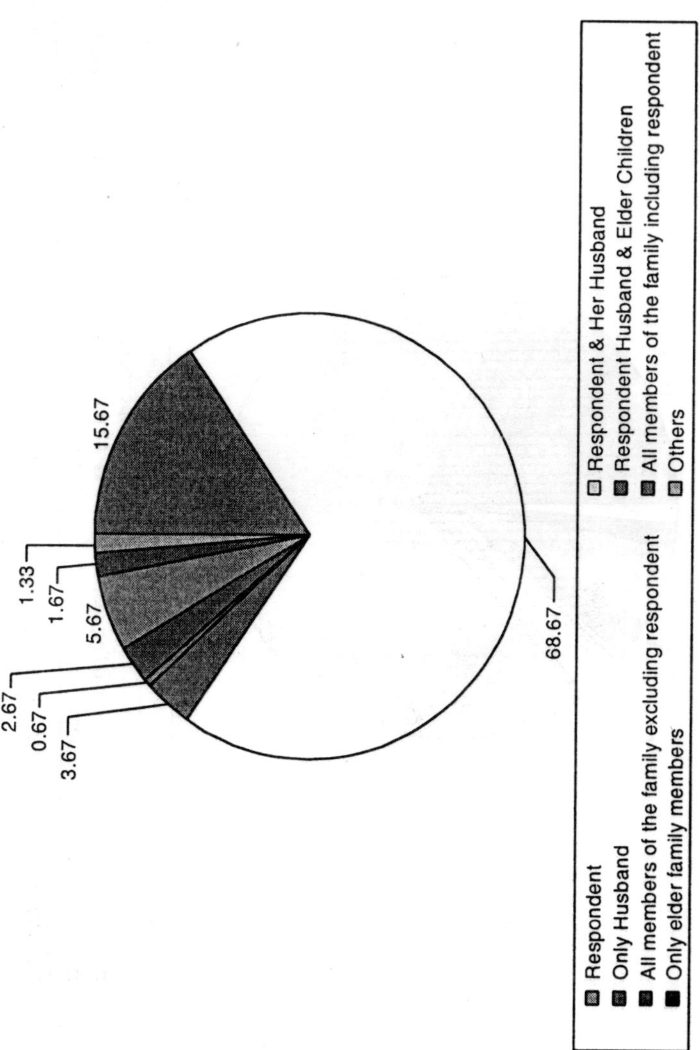

Fig. 5c Distribution of the respondents according to the decision making in the family

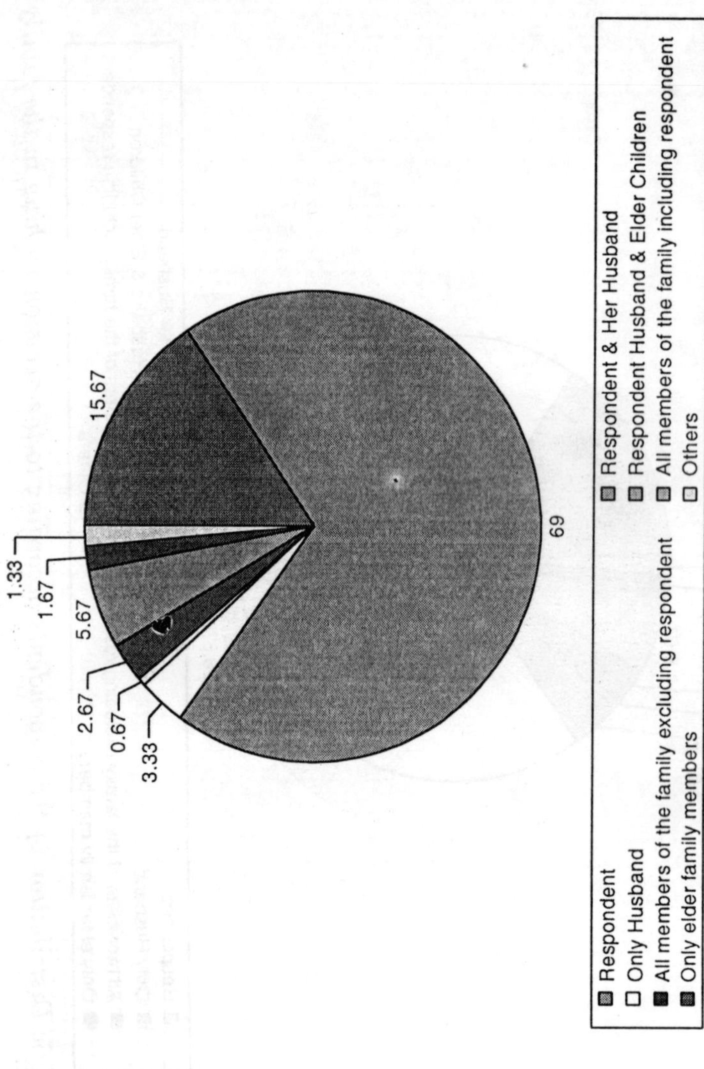

Fig. 5d Distribution of the respondents according to the decision making in the family

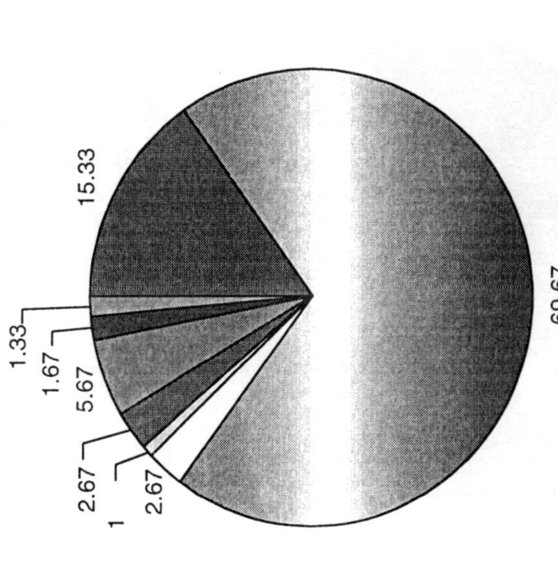

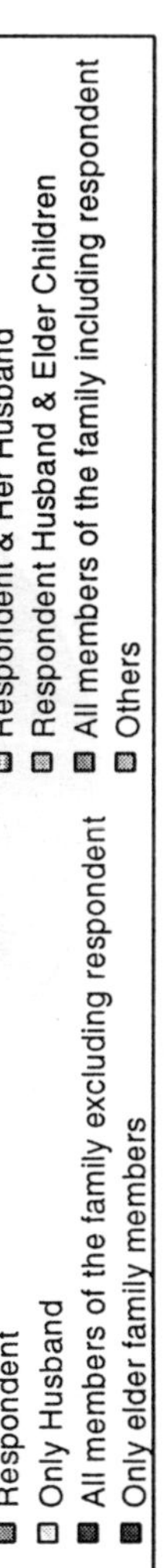

Fig. 5e Distribution of the respondents according to the decision making in the family

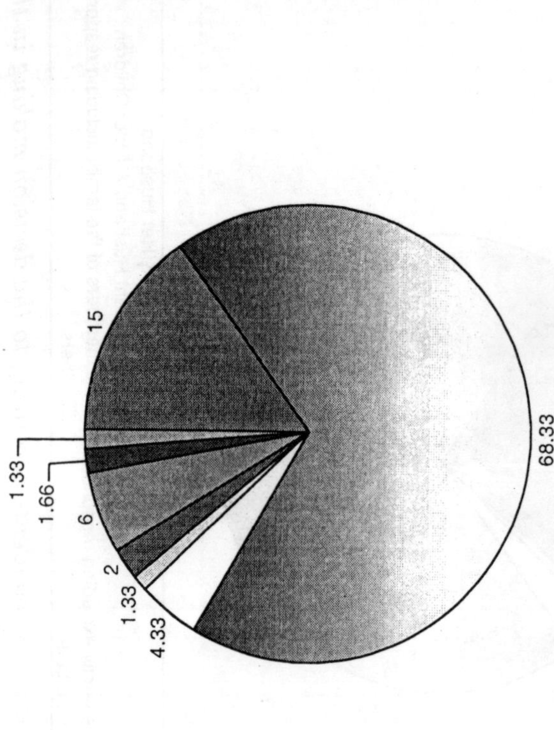

Fig. 5f Distribution of the respondents according to the decision making in the family

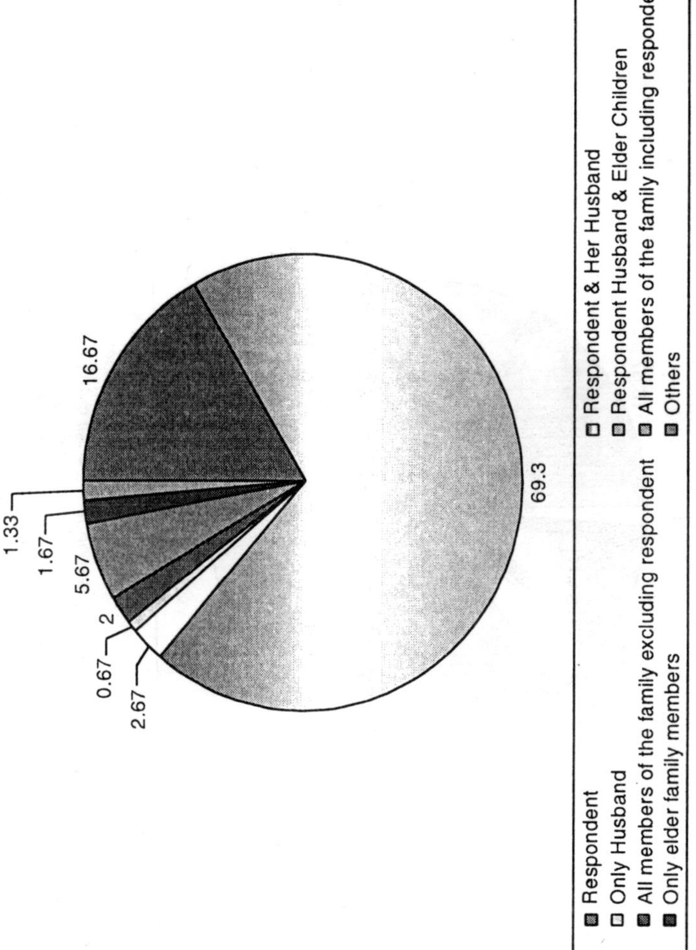

Fig. 5g Distribution of the respondents according to the decision making in the family

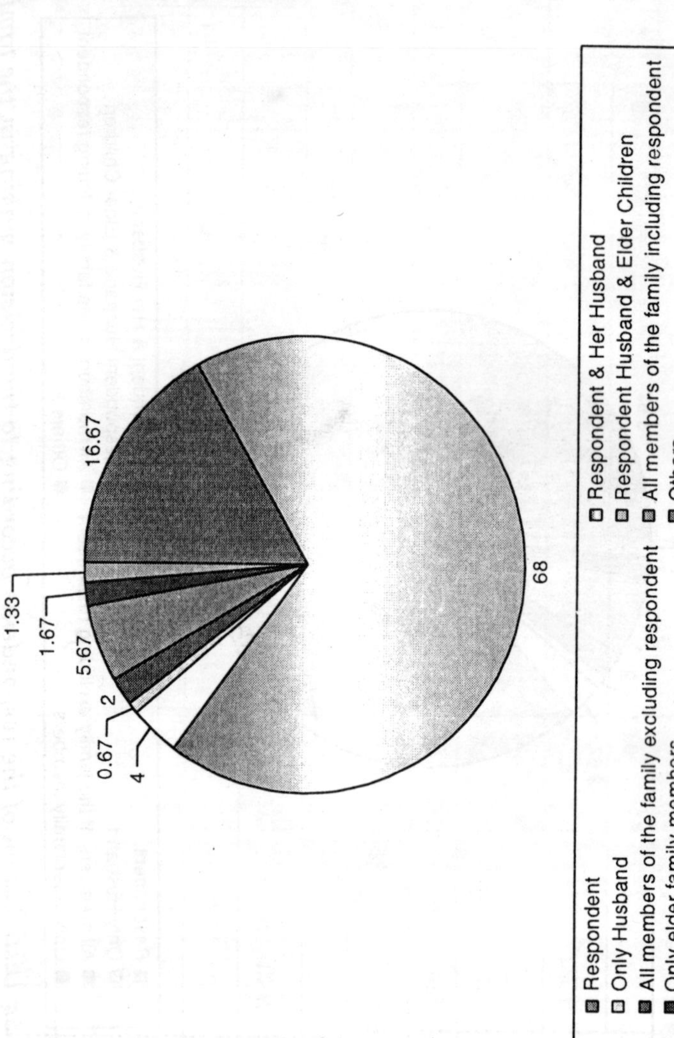

Fig. 5h Distribution of the respondents according to the decision making in the family

Table—4.18. Distribution of the respondents according to their assets

Assets (Movable & Immovable)	TRD				CRD				MRD				Total	Percentage (%)
	RGM	SKM	PKM	VPM	CTM	VDM	NVM	IRM	CGM	MPM	KVM	KPM		
Yes	22	25	23	25	24	20	23	23	24	20	24	22	275	91.67
No	3	—	2	—	1	5	2	2	1	5	1	3	25	8.33
Total	**25**	**25**	**25**	**25**	**25**	**25**	**25**	**25**	**25**	**25**	**25**	**25**	**300**	**100.00**

Table—4.18A

Assets	TRD				CRD				MRD				Total	Percentage (%)
	RGM	SKM	PKM	VPM	CTM	VDM	NVM	IRM	CGM	MPM	KVM	KPM		
1	*2*	*3*	*4*	*5*	*6*	*7*	*8*	*9*	*10*	*11*	*12*	*13*	*14*	*15*
						I Land Assets								
Yes	10	12	11	11	19	10	25	17	14	6	14	3	152	50.67
No	15	13	14	14	6	15	—	8	11	19	11	22	148	49.33
Total	**25**	**25**	**25**	**25**	**25**	**25**	**25**	**25**	**25**	**25**	**25**	**25**	**300**	**100.00**

II House Assets														
Yes	16	22	20	23	23	18	22	22	24	19	22	22	253	84.33
No	9	3	5	2	2	7	3	3	1	6	3	3	47	15.67
Total	**25**	**25**	**25**	**25**	**25**	**25**	**25**	**25**	**25**	**25**	**25**	**25**	**300**	**100.00**
III House Sites														
Yes	16	18	19	21	—	13	—	—	—	6	3	—	96	32
No	9	7	6	4	25	12	25	25	25	19	22	25	204	68
Total	**25**	**25**	**25**	**25**	**25**	**25**	**25**	**25**	**25**	**25**	**25**	**25**	**300**	**100.00**
IV Domestic Milch Animals														
Yes	8	13	11	8	15	8	4	13	10	7	11	2	110	36.67
No	17	12	14	17	10	17	21	12	15	18	14	23	190	63.33
Total	**25**	**25**	**25**	**25**	**25**	**25**	**25**	**25**	**25**	**25**	**25**	**25**	**300**	**100.00**
V Any other specify														
Yes	—	—	—	1	—	1	—	—	—	—	—	—	2	0.67
No	25	25	25	24	25	24	25	25	25	25	25	25	298	99.33
Total	**25**	**25**	**25**	**25**	**25**	**25**	**25**	**25**	**25**	**25**	**25**	**25**	**300**	**100.00**

Table—4.19. Distribution of the respondents according to the amount of over all savings

Over all savings in Rs.	*TRD*				*CRD*				*MRD*				*Total*	*Percentage (%)*
	RGM	*SKM*	*PKM*	*VPM*	*CTM*	*VDM*	*NVM*	*IRM*	*CGM*	*MPM*	*KVM*	*KPM*		
<-10,000	3	—	2	3	3	4	2	2	1	3	11	8	42	14.00
10,000-20,000	6	2	6	3	6	3	3	6	1	3	5	3	47	15.67
20,000-30,000	8	4	8	6	7	7	14	7	6	3	6	4	80	26.67
30,000-40,000	5	7	3	6	4	6	4	5	8	1	3	3	55	18.33
40,000-50,000	2	6	3	2	3	3	—	3	6	4	—	2	34	11.33
50,000 & >	1	6	3	5	2	2	2	2	3	11	—	5	42	14.00
Total	**25**	**25**	**25**	**25**	**25**	**25**	**25**	**25**	**25**	**25**	**25**	**25**	**300**	**100.00**

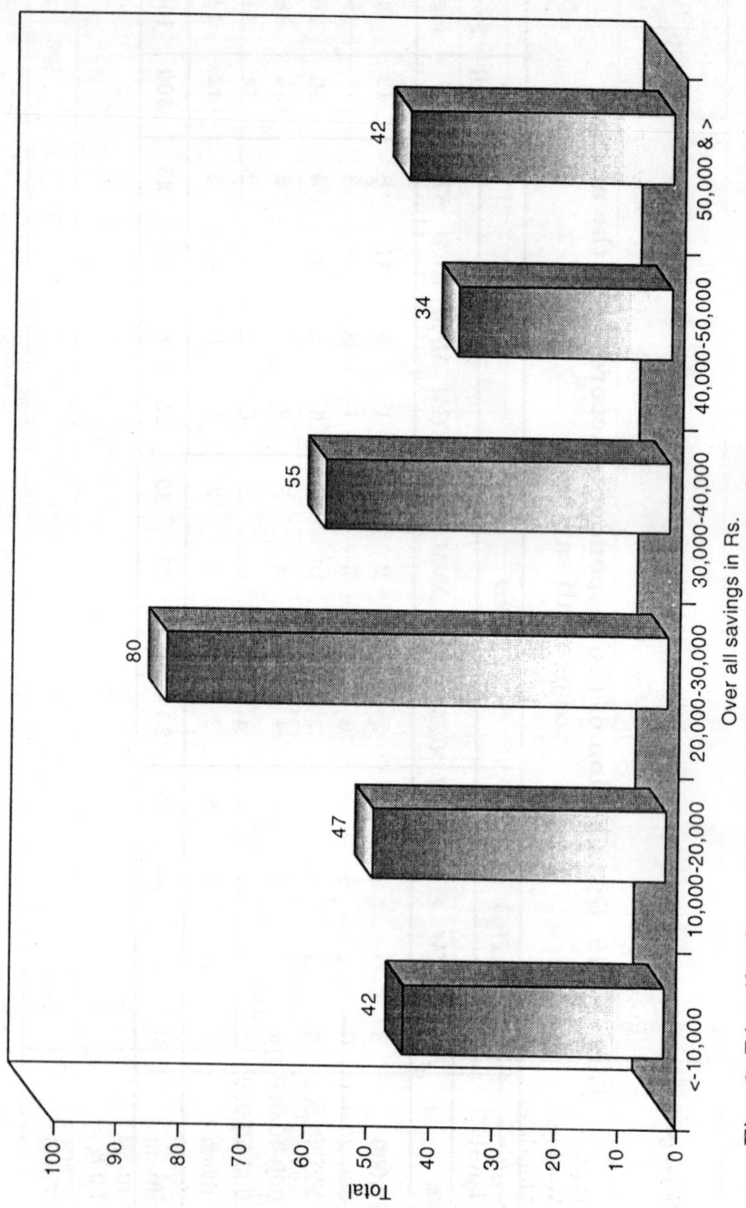

Fig. 6. Distribution of the respondents according to the amount of over all savings

Table—4.20. Distribution of the respondents according to their savings

Savings	*TRD*				*CRD*				*MRD*				*Total*	*Percentage (%)*
	RGM	*SKM*	*PKM*	*VPM*	*CTM*	*VDM*	*NVM*	*IRM*	*CGM*	*MPM*	*KVM*	*KPM*		
Daily	—	—	—	—	—	—	—	—	—	—	—	—	—	—
Weekly	—	—	—	—	—	—	—	—	—	—	—	4	4	1.33
Monthly	25	25	25	25	25	25	25	25	25	25	25	21	296	98.67
Total	**25**	**25**	**25**	**25**	**25**	**25**	**25**	**25**	**25**	**25**	**25**	**25**	**300**	**100.00**

Table—4.21. Distribution of the respondents according to their amount of savings per month

Amount of saving P/M in Rs.	*TRD*				*CRD*				*MRD*				*Total*	*Percentage (%)*
	RGM	*SKM*	*PKM*	*VPM*	*CTM*	*VDM*	*NVM*	*IRM*	*CGM*	*MPM*	*KVM*	*KPM*		
10-20	—	—	—	—	—	—	—	—	—	—	—	—	—	—
20-30	—	—	—	—	—	—	—	—	—	—	—	—	—	—
30-40	7	3	20	14	24	8	21	23	1	8	17	14	160	53.33
40-50	—	—	—	—	—	—	—	—	—	—	—	1	1	0.33
50 & >	18	22	5	11	1	17	4	2	24	17	8	10	139	46.33
Total	**25**	**25**	**25**	**25**	**25**	**25**	**25**	**25**	**25**	**25**	**25**	**25**	**300**	**100.00**

Table—4.22. Distribution of the respondents according to the maintenance of records of their savings

Records for savings	*TRD*				*CRD*				*MRD*				*Total*	*Percen-tage (%)*
	RGM	*SKM*	*PKM*	*VPM*	*CTM*	*VDM*	*NVM*	*IRM*	*CGM*	*MPM*	*KVM*	*KPM*		
Yes	25	25	25	25	25	25	25	25	25	25	25	25	300	100.00
No	—	—	—	—	—	—	—	—	—	—	—	—	—	—
Total	**25**	**25**	**25**	**25**	**25**	**25**	**25**	**25**	**25**	**25**	**25**	**25**	**300**	**100.00**

Table—4.23. Distribution of the respondents according to their debts

Debts	*TRD*				*CRD*				*MRD*				*Total*	*Percen-tage (%)*
	RGM	*SKM*	*PKM*	*VPM*	*CTM*	*VDM*	*NVM*	*IRM*	*CGM*	*MPM*	*KVM*	*KPM*		
Yes	23	24	23	24	22	23	22	22	23	22	19	24	271	90.33
No	2	1	2	1	3	2	3	3	2	3	6	1	29	9.67
Total	**25**	**25**	**25**	**25**	**25**	**25**	**25**	**25**	**25**	**25**	**25**	**25**	**300**	**100.00**

Table—24. Distribution of the respondents according to the source of debts

Source of Debts	*TRD*				*CRD*				*MRD*				*Total*	*Percentage (%)*
	RGM	*SKM*	*PKM*	*VPM*	*CTM*	*VDM*	*NVM*	*IRM*	*CGM*	*MPM*	*KVM*	*KPM*		
Bank	1	2	8	6	11	3	9	6	10	8	6	9	79	26.33
Money lender	3	—	—	—	—	3	—	—	—	—	—	—	6	2.00
Friends	3	1	—	1	—	3	—	1	—	—	—	—	9	3.00
Family source	—	—	—	—	—	—	—	—	—	—	—	—	—	—
Hand loan	1	—	—	—	—	2	—	—	—	—	—	—	3	1.00
Private Individuals	7	6	—	8	—	7	—	—	—	—	—	—	28	9.33
Group members	7	15	16	9	11	5	13	15	13	14	13	15	146	48.67
Any other	3	1	1	1	3	2	3	3	2	3	6	1	29	9.67
Total	**25**	**25**	**25**	**25**	**25**	**25**	**25**	**25**	**25**	**25**	**25**	**25**	**300**	**100.00**

Table—4.25. Distribution of the respondents according to the repayment of debts

Repayment of Debts	*TRD*				*CRD*				*MRD*				*Total*	*Percen-tage (%)*
	RGM	*SKM*	*PKM*	*VPM*	*CTM*	*VDM*	*NVM*	*IRM*	*CGM*	*MPM*	*KVM*	*KPM*		
By installments out of savings occured	4	2	1	1	—	4	—	1	—	1	—	—	14	4.67
By doing hard work	14	21	23	22	22	14	22	20	22	21	19	22	242	80.67
Chit fund	3	1	—	1	—	4	—	—	—	—	—	—	9	3.00
By getting dowry for male child	—	—	—	—	—	—	—	1	—	—	—	—	1	0.33
House selling	2	—	—	—	—	1	—	—	—	—	—	—	3	1.00
Don't know	2	1	1	1	3	2	3	3	3	3	6	3	31	10.33
Total	**25**	**25**	**25**	**25**	**25**	**25**	**25**	**25**	**25**	**25**	**25**	**25**	**300**	**100.00**

Table—4.26. Distribution of the respondents according to the year of joining in SHG

Year	*TRD*				*CRD*				*MRD*				*Total*	*Percentage (%)*
	RGM	*SKM*	*PKM*	*VPM*	*CTM*	*VDM*	*NVM*	*IRM*	*CGM*	*MPM*	*KVM*	*KPM*		
1990-1995	—	1	1	—	—	—	—	—	—	—	—	—	2	0.67
1995-2000	20	23	15	12	22	21	22	22	22	17	13	15	224	74.67
2000-2005	5	1	9	13	3	4	3	3	3	8	12	10	74	24.67
Total	**25**	**25**	**25**	**25**	**25**	**25**	**25**	**25**	**25**	**25**	**25**	**25**	**300**	**100.00**

Table—4.27. Distribution of the respondents according to the number of members in each group

Number	*TRD*				*CRD*				*MRD*				*Total*	*Percentage (%)*
	RGM	*SKM*	*PKM*	*VPM*	*CTM*	*VDM*	*NVM*	*IRM*	*CGM*	*MPM*	*KVM*	*KPM*		
10	1	—	—	—	—	1	3	—	—	5	1	2	13	4.33
10-15	14	16	12	14	18	17	17	17	23	18	23	9	198	66.00
15-20	10	9	13	11	7	7	5	8	2	2	1	14	89	29.67
Total	**25**	**25**	**25**	**25**	**25**	**25**	**25**	**25**	**25**	**25**	**25**	**25**	**300**	**100.00**

The above Table-4.26 shows that of the total respondents, 224 respondents (74.67 per cent) joined in SHGs in the year 1995-2000. It shows that maximum number of women joined in SHGs during the above period due to the several steps taken up by the government of Andhra Pradesh for the development/empowerment of women. 74 respondents (24.67 per cent) joined in SHGs during 2000-2005.

Table-4.27 shows distribution of the respondents according to the number of members in each group. According to the data, 198 respondents (66 per cent) told that there are 10-15 members in each group, 89 respondents (29.67 per cent) said that there are 15-20 members in each group and 13 respondents (4.33 per cent) told that there are 10 members in each group.

The data in Table-4.28 shows the distribution of the respondents according to their confidence before joining in SHG. According to the data, 162 respondents (54 per cent) have no confidence when they first joined in SHG, followed by 88 respondents (29.33 per cent) have very little confidence when they joined in SHG, 33 respondents (11 per cent) have little confidence when they joined in SHG, 9 respondents (3 per cent) had somewhat confidence and 8 respondents (2.67 per cent) had average confidence when they first joined in SHG.

Table-4.29 shows distribution of the respondents according to their opinion on social/economic status before joining SHG. According to the data, 289 respondents (96.33 per cent) opined that their status was lower in the society earlier.

Table-4.30 shows distribution of the respondents according to their opinion on social/economic status after joining SHG. According to the data, 230 respondents (76.67 per cent) told that their status is improved and high, followed by 64 respondents (21.33 per cent) told that their status is some what higher and six respondents (2 per cent) told that there is no change in their social and economic status.

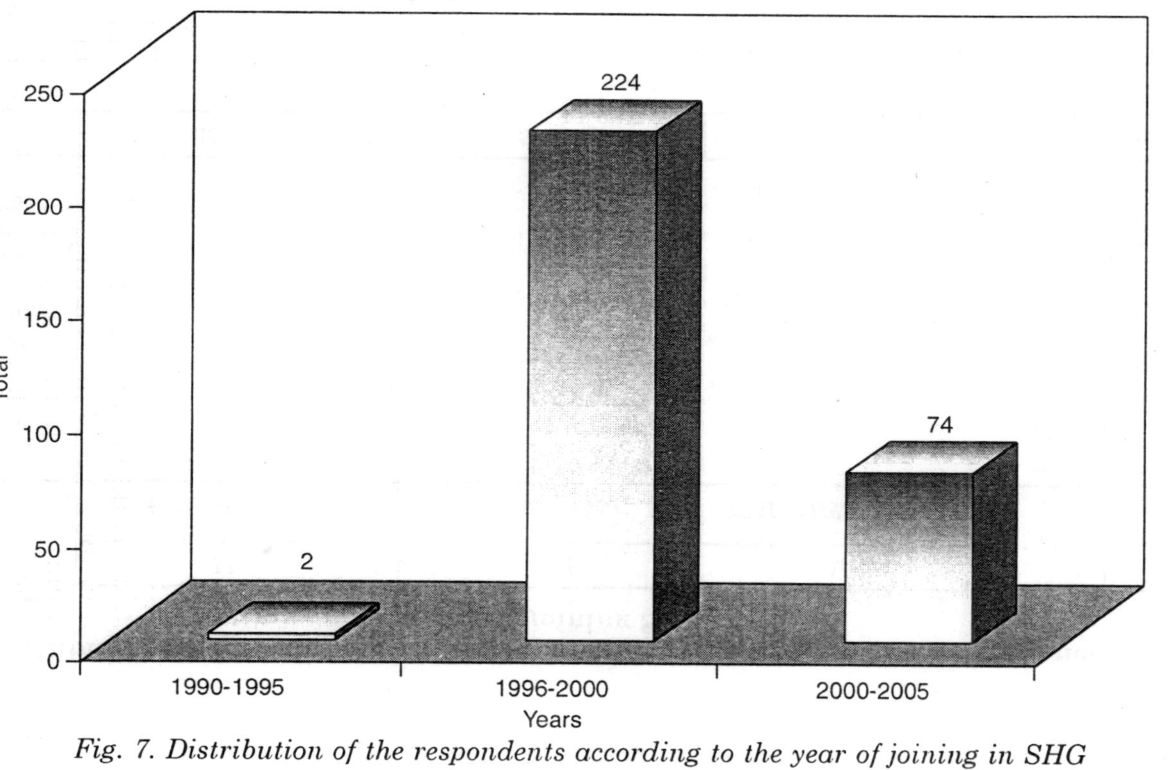

Fig. 7. Distribution of the respondents according to the year of joining in SHG

Table—4.28. Distribution of the respondents according to their confidence before joining SHG

Confident	*TRD*				*CRD*				*MRD*				*Total*	*Percen-tage (%)*
	RGM	*SKM*	*PKM*	*VPM*	*CTM*	*VDM*	*NVM*	*IRM*	*CGM*	*MPM*	*KVM*	*KPM*		
Very confident	—	—	—	—	—	—	—	—	—	—	—	—	—	—
Some what confident	2	—	3	1	—	2	1	—	—	—	—	—	9	3.00
Average confident	3	—	—	—	—	3	—	—	—	1	—	1	8	2.67
Little confident	6	3	2	1	—	8	—	1	3	1	3	5	33	11.00
Very little confident	7	7	9	7	6	6	6	7	8	5	11	9	88	29.33
Nothing	7	15	11	16	19	6	18	17	14	18	11	10	162	54.00
Total	**25**	**25**	**25**	**25**	**25**	**25**	**25**	**25**	**25**	**25**	**25**	**25**	**300**	**100.00**

Table—4.29. Distribution of the respondents according to their opinion on their social/economic status before joining SHG

Social/ economic status	*TRD*				*CRD*				*MRD*				*Total*	*Percentage (%)*
	RGM	*SKM*	*PKM*	*VPM*	*CTM*	*VDM*	*NVM*	*IRM*	*CGM*	*MPM*	*KVM*	*KPM*		
Lower	24	22	24	23	25	23	25	25	24	25	24	25	289	96.33
Moderate	1	3	1	2	—	2	—	—	1	—	1	—	11	3.67
Total	**25**	**25**	**25**	**25**	**25**	**25**	**25**	**25**	**25**	**25**	**25**	**25**	**300**	**100.00**

Table—4.30. Distribution of the respondents according to their opinion on social/economic status after joining SHG

Opinion	*TRD*				*CRD*				*MRD*				*Total*	*Percentage (%)*
	RGM	*SKM*	*PKM*	*VPM*	*CTM*	*VDM*	*NVM*	*IRM*	*CGM*	*MPM*	*KVM*	*KPM*		
High	14	20	19	19	24	16	21	23	19	21	14	21	230	76.67
Some what higher	10	3	5	6	1	8	4	1	7	4	11	4	64	21.33
No change	1	2	1	—	—	1	—	1	—	—	—	—	6	2.00
Some what lower	—	—	—	—	—	—	—	—	—	—	—	—	—	—
Lower	—	—	—	—	—	—	—	—	—	—	—	—	—	—
Total	**25**	**25**	**25**	**25**	**25**	**25**	**25**	**25**	**25**	**25**	**25**	**25**	**300**	**100.00**

Table—4.31. Distribution of the respondents according to the sources of knowing this programme

Sources	*TRD*				*CRD*				*MRD*				*Total*	*Percen-tage (%)*
	RGM	*SKM*	*PKM*	*VPM*	*CTM*	*VDM*	*NVM*	*IRM*	*CGM*	*MPM*	*KVM*	*KPM*		
MPDO	13	4	9	15	3	14	1	3	5	1	3	14	85	28.33
Extension officer	—	—	2	—	—	—	2	—	8	—	3	3	18	6.00
School teacher	1	1	—	1	3	1	—	3	1	1	—	—	12	4.00
Neighbours	8	20	5	9	16	7	20	14	9	10	4	8	130	43.33
NGO's	3	—	6	—	3	3	2	3	—	—	11	—	31	10.33
VDO	—	—	3	—	—	—	—	2	2	13	4	—	24	8.00
Total	25	25	25	25	25	25	25	25	25	25	25	25	300	100.00

Table-4.31 shows distribution of the respondents according to the sources of knowing this programme. According to the data, 130 respondents (43.33 per cent) came to know about this programme from neighbours, followed by 85 respondents (28.33 per cent) from MPDO and 10.33 per cent from NGO's. The rest of the respondents came to know about this programme from extension officer, school teacher and VDO.

Table-4.32 shows distribution of the respondents according to the reasons for joining in the programme. According to the data, 214 respondents (71.33 per cent) expressed that they have joined in this programme to supplement their family income, followed by 75 respondents (25 per cent) as a source of income. The rest of the respondents expressed that it is more suitable to women to use their fiscal talents in a better manner and Deepam Pathakam.

Not only the reasons for join the programme, but also the data regarding the motivational factors to join women in SHGs is also collected. The main Motivational factor "To earn money" is motivated 285 respondents (95 per cent) to join in SHG, followed by 15 respondents (5 per cent) to become empowered and famous.

Table-4.34 shows distribution of the respondents according to the compelling reasons influenced to join in SHG. According to the data, 181 respondents (60.33 per cent) joined in SHG because of the family burdens followed by 88 respondents (29.33 per cent) joined SHG to lead a better life, 24 respondents (8 per cent) to help the family and to assist the husband for income generation and 7 respondents (2.33 per cent) joined in SHG due to unemployment.

Table-4.35 shows distribution of the respondents according to the personnel who motivated women to join in the programme. According to the data, 119 respondents (39.67 per cent) are motivated by their Neighbours, followed by 56 respondents (18.67 per cent) motivated by VDO and 56 respondents (18.67 per cent) motivated by MPDO's, 26 respondents (8.67 per cent) motivated by Sangamitra/ Velugu Community Co-ordinators and 24 respondents (8.00 per cent) are motivated by Non Governmental Organizations. The remaining respondents are motivated by relatives, extension officer and sarpanch.

Table—4.32. Distribution of the respondents according to the reasons for join the programme

Reasons	*TRD*				*CRD*				*MRD*				*Total*	*Percen-tage (%)*
	RGM	*SKM*	*PKM*	*VPM*	*CTM*	*VDM*	*NVM*	*IRM*	*CGM*	*MPM*	*KVM*	*KPM*		
To supplement family income	21	24	21	25	6	19	18	6	21	22	13	18	214	71.33
As a source of income	2	—	—	—	19	3	7	19	4	3	11	7	75	25.00
It is more suitable to women	1	—	2	—	—	1	—	—	—	—	1	—	5	1.67
To use fiscal talents in a better manner	—	1	2	—	—	—	—	—	—	—	—	—	3	1.00
Deepam pathakam	1	—	—	—	—	2	—	—	—	—	—	—	3	1.00
Total	**25**	**25**	**25**	**25**	**25**	**25**	**25**	**25**	**25**	**25**	**25**	**25**	**300**	**100.00**

Table—4.33. Distribution of the respondents according to the motivational factors to join in SHG

Motivational factors	*TRD*				*CRD*				*MRD*				*Total*	*Percentage (%)*
	RGM	*SKM*	*PKM*	*VPM*	*CTM*	*VDM*	*NVM*	*IRM*	*CGM*	*MPM*	*KVM*	*KPM*		
To earn money	22	24	21	25	25	22	25	25	24	24	23	25	285	95.00
To become empowered and famous	3	1	4	—	—	3	—	—	1	1	2	—	15	5.00
Total	**25**	**25**	**25**	**25**	**25**	**25**	**25**	**25**	**25**	**25**	**25**	**25**	**300**	**100.00**

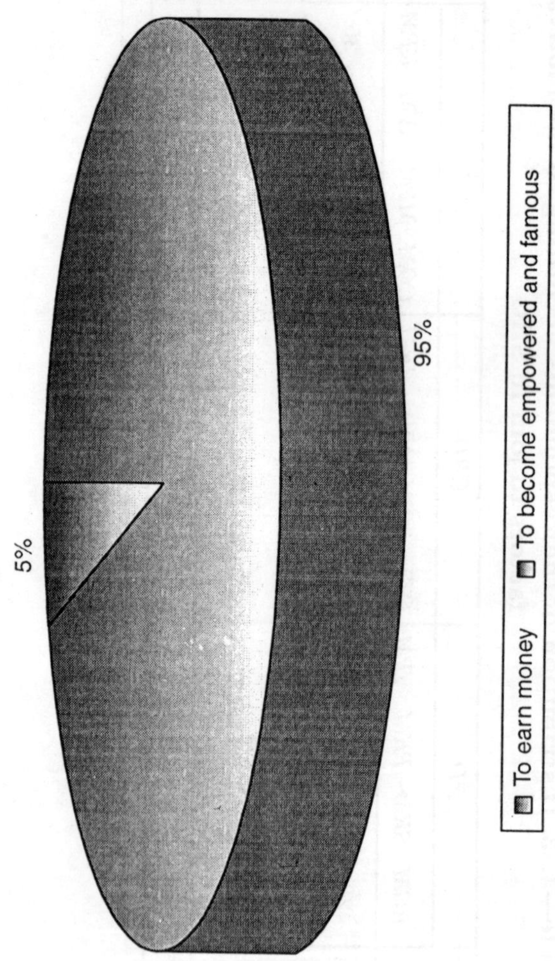

Fig. 8. Distribution of the respondents according to the motivational factors to join in SHG

Table—4.34. Distribution of the respondents according to the compelling reasons influenced to join in SHG

Compelling reasons	*TRD*				*CRD*				*MRD*				*Total*	*Percentage (%)*
	RGM	*SKM*	*PKM*	*VPM*	*CTM*	*VDM*	*NVM*	*IRM*	*CGM*	*MPM*	*KVM*	*KPM*		
Unemployment	2	2	2	—	—	1	—	—	—	—	—	—	7	2.33
To lead a better life	12	13	11	12	2	13	—	2	4	6	6	7	88	29.33
Family burdens	4	9	10	13	23	5	25	22	20	15	17	18	181	60.33
To help the family and to assist the husband for income generation	7	1	2	—	—	6	—	1	1	4	2	—	24	8.00
Total	**25**	**25**	**25**	**25**	**25**	**25**	**25**	**25**	**25**	**25**	**25**	**25**	**300**	**100.00**

Table—4.35. Distribution of the respondents according to the personnel who motivated women to join the programme

Personnel	*TRD*				*CRD*				*MRD*				*Total*	*Percen-tage (%)*
	RGM	*SKM*	*PKM*	*VPM*	*CTM*	*VDM*	*NVM*	*IRM*	*CGM*	*MPM*	*KVM*	*KPM*		
Neighbours	7	17	10	16	13	7	9	15	9	11	—	5	119	39.67
Relatives	—	—	—	—	1	—	—	1	—	—	—	1	3	1.00
Extension Officer	—	1	—	—	—	—	2	—	6	—	3	2	14	4.67
VDO	2	1	6	3	7	4	7	5	1	13	4	3	56	18.67
Sarpanch	—	—	—	—	—	—	1	—	—	—	—	1	2	0.67
MPDO	12	2	6	4	2	11	1	2	7	—	—	9	56	18.67
NGO's	2	—	2	—	—	2	2	—	—	—	12	4	24	8.00
Velugu CC/ Sangamitra/ Any other	2	4	1	2	2	1	3	2	2	1	6	—	26	8.67
Total	**25**	**25**	**25**	**25**	**25**	**25**	**25**	**25**	**25**	**25**	**25**	**25**	**300**	**100.00**

Table—4.36. Distribution of the respondents according to the person who supervise/monitor group activities

Person	*TRD*				*CRD*				*MRD*				*Total*	*Percen-tage (%)*
	RGM	*SKM*	*PKM*	*VPM*	*CTM*	*VDM*	*NVM*	*IRM*	*CGM*	*MPM*	*KVM*	*KPM*		
MPDO	—	—	—	—	—	1	—	—	1	—	—	1	3	0.99
VAO/VDO	—	12	—	—	—	—	—	—	—	—	2	—	14	4.67
Village secretary	2	2	4	—	2	4	1	3	—	4	5	3	30	10.00
Representatives of NGO	2	—	3	—	—	2	2	—	—	—	8	8	25	8.33
Sangamitra	18	8	17	21	22	17	22	22	24	21	3	12	207	69.00
Velugu CC & CA	—	—	—	—	—	—	—	—	—	—	6	1	7	2.33
Other group leader	3	3	1	4	—	1	—	—	—	—	—	—	12	4.00
None	—	—	—	—	1	—	—	—	—	—	1	—	2	0.67
Total	**25**	**25**	**25**	**25**	**25**	**25**	**25**	**25**	**25**	**25**	**25**	**25**	**300**	**100.00**

Table-4.36 shows distribution of the respondents according to the person who supervise/monitor the group activities. According to the data, 207 respondents (69 per cent) expressed that the group activities are supervise/ monitor by Sangamitra, followed by 30 respondents (10 per cent) expressed that the group activities are supervise/ monitor by village secretary, 25 respondents (8.33 per cent) expressed that the group activities are supervise/monitor by representatives of NGO's. The rest of the respondents told that the group activities are supervise/monitor by MPDO, VAO/VDO, and Velugu CC & CA and only two respondents (0.67 per cent) said that nobody supervise/monitor the group activities.

Table-4.37 shows the government officials visit to the SHG groups. According to the data, 168 respondents (56 per cent) told that monthly once the government officials visit the SHG groups and 110 respondents (36.67 per cent) told that the government officials visit rarely. The rest of them told that the government officials visit SHG groups weekly once or monthly twice.

Table-4.38 shows distribution of the respondents according to the selection of the group leaders. According to the data, 116 respondents (39 per cent) select their group leader basing on educational qualification, followed by 96 respondents (32 per cent) select their group leader if she is co-operative and faithful person, and 83 respondents (27.67 per cent) select their group leader if she is dynamic.

Table-4.39 shows activities attended by the respondents. As a SHG member the respondent must have participated in different activities. According to the data, 98.67 per cent of the respondents attended training programmes, 99.67 per cent of the respondents attended group meetings regularly and 2.33 per cent of the respondents attended field work/ melas/DWCRA Bazaars.

The data in Table-4.40 shows distribution of the respondents according to the person who conduct the meetings. According to the data, 288 respondents (96 per cent) told that group leader will conduct the meetings, 9 respondents (3 per cent) told Sangamitras and three respondents (1 per cent) told NGO's will conduct the meetings. The group leader has the primary duty to conduct the group meetings.

Table—4.37. Distribution of the respondents according to the Government officials visit to the SHGs

Govt. officials	TRD				CRD				MRD				Total	Percentage (%)
	RGM	SKM	PKM	VPM	CTM	VDM	NVM	IRM	CGM	MPM	KVM	KPM		
Weekly once	1	—	—	—	1	1	1	1	—	—	—	4	9	3.00
Monthly once	24	25	3	7	17	22	—	17	6	25	7	15	168	4.00
Monthly twice	—	—	—	—	6	—	—	5	—	—	—	1	12	56.00
Rare	—	—	22	17	1	2	24	2	19	—	18	5	110	36.67
Any other (specify)	—	—	—	1	—	—	—	—	—	—	—	—	1	0.33
Total	**25**	**25**	**25**	**25**	**25**	**25**	**25**	**25**	**25**	**25**	**25**	**25**	**300**	**100.00**

Table—4.38. Distribution of the respondents according to the selection of the group leader

Selection of the group leader	TRD				CRD				MRD				Total	Percentage (%)
	RGM	SKM	PKM	VPM	CTM	VDM	NVM	IRM	CGM	MPM	KVM	KPM		
Education	12	9	9	7	7	13	17	7	14	10	8	4	117	39.00
Dynamic	6	4	11	3	5	6	—	5	3	9	11	20	83	27.67
Sportive	—	—	—	—	1	1	1	1	—	—	—	—	4	1.33
Co-operative & Faithful	7	12	5	15	12	5	7	12	8	6	6	1	96	32.00
Total	**25**	**25**	**25**	**25**	**25**	**25**	**25**	**25**	**25**	**25**	**25**	**25**	**300**	**100.00**

Table—4.39. Distribution of the respondents according to their activities attended

Activities	*TRD*				*CRD*				*MRD*				*Total*	*Percentage (%)*
	RGM	*SKM*	*PKM*	*VPM*	*CTM*	*VDM*	*NVM*	*IRM*	*CGM*	*MPM*	*KVM*	*KPM*		
Training														
Yes	23	25	25	25	25	24	25	24	25	25	25	25	296	98.67
No	2	—	—	—	—	1	—	1	—	—	—	—	4	1.33
Total	**25**	**25**	**25**	**25**	**25**	**25**	**25**	**25**	**25**	**25**	**25**	**25**	**300**	**100.00**
Group Meeting														
Yes	24	25	25	25	25	25	25	25	25	25	25	25	299	99.67
No	1	—	—	—	—	—	—	—	—	—	—	—	1	0.33
Total	**25**	**25**	**25**	**25**	**25**	**25**	**25**	**25**	**25**	**25**	**25**	**25**	**300**	**100.00**
Field work/Mela/DWCRA Bazaar														
Yes	4	1	—	—	—	1	—	—	1	—	—	—	7	2.33
No	21	24	25	25	25	24	25	25	24	25	25	25	293	97.67
Total	**25**	**25**	**25**	**25**	**25**	**25**	**25**	**25**	**25**	**25**	**25**	**25**	**300**	**100.00**

(Contd.)

Activities	TRD				CRD				MRD				Total	Percentage (%)
	RGM	SKM	PKM	VPM	CTM	VDM	NVM	IRM	CGM	MPM	KVM	KPM		
Any other														
Yes	—	—	—	—	—	—	—	—	—	—	—	—	—	—
No	25	25	25	25	25	25	25	25	25	25	25	25	300	100.00
Total	25	25	25	25	25	25	25	25	25	25	25	25	300	100.00

Table—4.40. Distribution of the respondents according to the person who conduct the meetings

Person	TRD				CRD				MRD				Total	Percentage (%)
	RGM	SKM	PKM	VPM	CTM	VDM	NVM	IRM	CGM	MPM	KVM	KPM		
Group leader	19	25	25	22	25	23	25	25	25	24	25	25	288	96.00
NGO's	2	—	—	—	—	1	—	—	—	—	—	—	3	1.00
Sangamitra	4	—	—	3	—	1	—	—	—	1	—	—	9	3.00
Total	**25**	**25**	**25**	**25**	**25**	**25**	**25**	**25**	**25**	**25**	**25**	**25**	**300**	**100.00**

Table—4.41. Distribution of the respondents according to the group meetings

Meeting	*TRD*				*CRD*				*MRD*				*Total*	*Percentage (%)*
	RGM	*SKM*	*PKM*	*VPM*	*CTM*	*VDM*	*NVM*	*IRM*	*CGM*	*MPM*	*KVM*	*KPM*		
Weekly	—	—	—	—	—	—	—	—	—	—	5	3	8	2.67
Fortnightly	1	—	—	8	—	—	3	—	—	—	—	—	12	4.00
Monthly	24	25	25	17	25	25	22	25	25	25	20	22	280	93.33
Total	**25**	**25**	**25**	**25**	**25**	**25**	**25**	**25**	**25**	**25**	**25**	**25**	**300**	**100.00**

Table—4.42. Distribution of the respondents according to the place of meeting

Place	*TRD*				*CRD*				*MRD*				*Total*	*Percentage (%)*
.	*RGM*	*SKM*	*PKM*	*VPM*	*CTM*	*VDM*	*NVM*	*IRM*	*CGM*	*MPM*	*KVM*	*KPM*		
Leaders house	11	12	2	3	8	12	23	8	15	13	16	15	138	46.00
Temple	11	9	22	15	7	11	1	14	8	2	4	4	108	36.00
Community Hall	2	—	—	—	7	2	1	1	—	—	2	—	15	5.00
School	1	4	1	7	3	—	—	2	2	10	3	6	39	13.00
Total	**25**	**25**	**25**	**25**	**25**	**25**	**25**	**25**	**25**	**25**	**25**	**25**	**300**	**100.00**

Table-4.41 shows distribution of the respondents according to the group meetings. Conduct of group meetings is most important in SHG's. According to the data, 280 respondents (93.33 per cent) attend the meetings monthly, 12 respondents (4 per cent) attend fortnightly and 8 respondents (2.66 per cent) attend the meetings weekly.

Table-4.42 shows distribution of the respondents according to the place of meetings. According to the data, 138 respondents (46 per cent) meet in the residence of group leader. 108 respondents (36 per cent) meet in temple, 39 respondents (13 per cent) meet in school and 15 respondents (5 per cent) meet in community hall whenever they have meetings.

Table-4.43 shows distribution of the respondents according to the discussion of topics in meetings. According to the data, 143 respondents (47.67 per cent) told that they discuss about members sincerity in savings and attendance, followed by 140 respondents (46.67 per cent) that they discuss all matters related to the family and community in the group meetings.

Table-4.44 shows distribution of the respondents according to the maintenance of accounts. According to the data, 221 respondents (73.67 per cent) told that group leaders are maintaining accounts for their savings followed by 39 respondents (13 per cent) that Sangamitra/ Accountants are maintaining accounts for their savings and 19 respondents (6.33 per cent) that other groups leaders are maintaining accounts for their savings. The rest of the respondents told that NGO's organisor are maintaining records for their savings.

Table-4.45 shows the amount of matching grant received by the SHG women. According to the data, 80 respondents (26.67 per cent) have taken the matching grant from Rs. 5,000-15,000. 28 respondents (9.33 per cent) Rs. 15,000-20000 and 20 respondents (6.67 per cent) have taken the matching grant amount of Rs. 25,000-30,000 and only one respondent (0.33 per cent) have taken the matching grant amount below Rs. 5,000.

Table—4.43. Distribution of the respondents according to the discussion of topics in meetings

Topics	*TRD*				*CRD*				*MRD*				*Total*	*Percentage (%)*
	RGM	*SKM*	*PKM*	*VPM*	*CTM*	*VDM*	*NVM*	*IRM*	*CGM*	*MPM*	*KVM*	*KPM*		
Cleanliness/ Sanitation	—	—	—	—	—	—	—	—	—	1	5	—	6	2.00
Small family norm and Adoption of F.P.	—	—	—	—	—	—	—	—	1	—	—	—	1	0.33
Drainage facilities	—	—	1	—	—	—	—	—	—	—	—	—	1	0.33
Sincerity in savings and attendance	9	17	15	14	12	10	11	11	8	14	9	13	143	47.67
Family problems	1	—	2	—	1	2	—	1	—	—	2	—	9	3.00
Above all	15	8	7	11	12	13	14	13	16	10	9	12	140	46.67
Total	**25**	**25**	**25**	**25**	**25**	**25**	**25**	**25**	**25**	**25**	**25**	**25**	**300**	**100.00**

Table—4.44. Distribution of the respondents according to the maintenance of accounts

Maintenance of Accounts	*TRD*				*CRD*				*MRD*				*Total*	*Percen-tage (%)*
	RGM	*SKM*	*PKM*	*VPM*	*CTM*	*VDM*	*NVM*	*IRM*	*CGM*	*MPM*	*KVM*	*KPM*		
Group leader	16	22	23	14	17	19	23	18	23	25	23	11	234	78.00
Other group leader	1	3	—	3	3	—	—	1	1	—	2	5	19	6.33
NGO's organisor	2	—	1	—	—	2	—	—	—	—	—	3	8	2.67
Sangamitra/ Accountant	6	—	1	8	5	4	2	6	1	—	—	6	39	13.00
Total	**25**	**25**	**25**	**25**	**25**	**25**	**25**	**25**	**25**	**25**	**25**	**25**	**300**	**100.00**

Table—4.45. Distribution of the respondents according to the amount of matching grant

Accounts	*TRD*				*CRD*				*MRD*				*Total*	*Percen-tage (%)*
	RGM	*SKM*	*PKM*	*VPM*	*CTM*	*VDM*	*NVM*	*IRM*	*CGM*	*MPM*	*KVM*	*KPM*		
<5000	—	—	—	—	—	—	—	1	—	—	—	—	1	0.33
5000-10000	3	9	5	7	13	7	6	13	11	—	3	3	80	26.67
10000-15000	11	8	6	11	6	5	6	2	7	6	8	4	80	26.67
15000-20000	4	3	5	1	—	2	2	1	2	4	—	4	28	9.33
20000-25000	—	—	—	—	—	—	—	—	—	—	—	—	—	—
25000-30000	2	2	1	1	1	1	—	1	3	7	—	1	20	6.67
Total	**20**	**22**	**17**	**20**	**20**	**15**	**14**	**18**	**23**	**17**	**11**	**12**	**209**	**69.64**

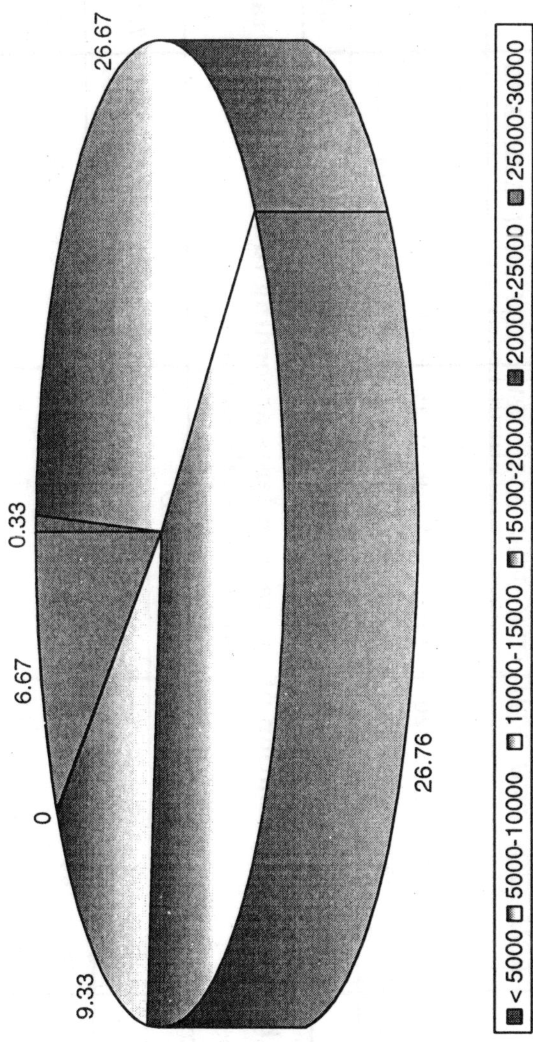

Fig. 9. Distribution of the respondent according to the amount of matching grant

Table—4.46. Distribution of the respondents according to the person who is giving matching grant to the savings

The person	*TRD*				*CRD*				*MRD*				*Total*	*Percen-tage (%)*
	RGM	*SKM*	*PKM*	*VPM*	*CTM*	*VDM*	*NVM*	*IRM*	*CGM*	*MPM*	*KVM*	*KPM*		
NGO's	1	1	—	—	6	—	5	1	—	—	4	1	19	6.33
DRDA	19	21	17	20	14	15	9	17	23	17	7	11	190	63.33
Not taken	5	3	8	5	5	10	11	7	2	8	14	13	91	30.33
Total	**25**	**25**	**25**	**25**	**25**	**25**	**25**	**25**	**25**	**25**	**25**	**25**	**300**	**100.00**

Table—4.47. Distribution of the respondents according to the facility of taking loans out of their savings

Facility	*TRD*				*CRD*				*MRD*				*Total*	*Percen-tage (%)*
	RGM	*SKM*	*PKM*	*VPM*	*CTM*	*VDM*	*NVM*	*IRM*	*CGM*	*MPM*	*KVM*	*KPM*		
Yes	20	22	22	17	23	21	18	22	22	21	15	18	241	80.33
No	5	3	3	8	2	4	7	3	3	4	10	7	59	19.67
Total	**25**	**25**	**25**	**25**	**25**	**25**	**25**	**25**	**25**	**25**	**25**	**25**	**300**	**100.00**

Table-4.46 shows the person who is giving matching grant to the savings. According to the data, 190 respondents (63.33 per cent) told that they have received matching grant from DRDA and 19 respondents (6.33 per cent) have expressed that they have taken matching grant from NGOs and 91 respondents (30.33 per cent) have not taken the matching grant from anybody.

Table-4.47 shows distribution of the respondents according to the facility of taking loans out of their savings. According to the data, 247 respondents (80.33 per cent) have utilised the facility of taking loans out of their savings and 59 respondents (19.67 per cent) have not utilised the facility of taking loans from their savings.

Table-4.48 shows distribution of the respondents according to the purpose of taking loans from the group found. According to the data, 59 respondents (19.67 per cent) have not utilised the facility of taking loans and 56 respondents (18.67 per cent) have taken loan from the group fund for the purpose of dairying, 54 respondents (18 per cent) have taken loan for the purpose of business, 48 respondents (16 per cent) have taken loan for domestic purpose, 37 respondents (12.33 per cent) have taken loan for the purpose of sheep/goat/cattle rearing and 21 respondents (7 per cent) have taken loan for the purpose of petty shop.

Table-4.49 shows distribution of the respondents according to the awareness of the government programmes. According to the data, 299 respondents (99.67 per cent) are aware of the government programmes and only one respondent (0.33 per cent) is not aware of the government programmes.

Table-4.50 shows distribution of the respondents according to their participation in governmental programmes. According to the data, 269 respondents (89.67 per cent) participated in Immunisation Programme, followed by 271 (90.33 per cent) respondents participated in Pulse Polio Programme, 275 respondents (91.67 per cent) participated in Literacy Programme and 298 respondents (99.33 per cent) participated in Janmabhoomi Programme and 226 respondents (75.33 per cent) participated in AIDS Awareness Programme in three revenue divisions and only five respondents (1.67 per cent) participated in other programmes.

Table—4.48. Distribution of the respondents according to the purpose of taking loans from the group fund

Purpose	*TRD*				*CRD*				*MRD*				*Total*	*Percentage (%)*
	RGM	*SKM*	*PKM*	*VPM*	*CTM*	*VDM*	*NVM*	*IRM*	*CGM*	*MPM*	*KVM*	*KPM*		
Dairying	5	10	2	7	8	3	—	7	5	3	3	3	56	18.67
Cultivation	—	6	—	—	—	—	1	—	—	1	—	—	8	2.67
Domestic purpose	4	3	9	2	—	3	5	1	6	—	8	7	48	16.00
Business	2	—	5	2	1	4	5	2	10	12	3	8	54	18.00
Sheep/Goat/ Cattle rearing	5	2	4	5	9	5	—	7	—	—	—	—	37	12.33
Petty shop	—	1	2	1	5	2	4	3	1	1	1	—	21	7.00
Regichembulu Tayaree	2	—	—	—	—	1	—	—	—	—	—	—	3	1.00
Tailoring/ Golisanchi	2	—	—	—	—	3	1	—	—	1	—	—	7	2.33
Small scale Industry	—	—	—	—	—	—	2	—	—	2	—	—	4	1.33

(Contd.)

Purpose	*TRD*				*CRD*				*MRD*				*Total*	*Percentage (%)*
	RGM	*SKM*	*PKM*	*VPM*	*CTM*	*VDM*	*NVM*	*IRM*	*CGM*	*MPM*	*KVM*	*KPM*		
Traditional occupation	—	—	—	—	—	—	—	2	—	1	—	—	3	1.00
No utilised purpose	5	3	3	8	2	4	7	3	3	4	10	7	59	19.67
Total	**25**	**25**	**25**	**25**	**25**	**25**	**25**	**25**	**25**	**25**	**25**	**25**	**300**	**100.00**

Table—4.49. Distribution of the respondents according to the awareness of the government programmes

Govt. programmes	*TRD*				*CRD*				*MRD*				*Total*	*Percentage (%)*
	RGM	*SKM*	*PKM*	*VPM*	*CTM*	*VDM*	*NVM*	*IRM*	*CGM*	*MPM*	*KVM*	*KPM*		
Yes	25	25	25	24	25	25	25	25	25	25	25	25	299	99.67
No	—	—	—	1	—	—	—	—	—	—	—	—	1	0.33
Total	**25**	**25**	**25**	**25**	**25**	**25**	**25**	**25**	**25**	**25**	**25**	**25**	**300**	**100.00**

Table—4.50. Distribution of the respondents according to their participation in governmental programmes

Governmental Programmes	*TRD*				*CRD*				*MRD*				*Total*	*Percentage (%)*
	RGM	*SKM*	*PKM*	*VPM*	*CTM*	*VDM*	*NVM*	*IRM*	*CGM*	*MPM*	*KVM*	*KPM*		
Yes	22	25	25	25	24	22	15	24	23	22	20	22	269	89.67
No	3	—	—	—	1	3	10	1	2	3	5	3	31	10.33
Total	**25**	**25**	**25**	**25**	**25**	**25**	**25**	**25**	**25**	**25**	**25**	**25**	**300**	**100.00**
Pulse polio programme														
Yes	22	25	25	25	24	22	17	24	23	22	20	22	271	90.33
No	3	—	—	—	1	3	8	1	2	3	5	3	29	9.67
Total	**25**	**25**	**25**	**25**	**25**	**25**	**25**	**25**	**25**	**25**	**25**	**25**	**300**	**100.00**
Literacy programme														
Yes	23	25	25	25	24	23	15	24	23	25	20	23	275	91.67
No	2	—	—	—	1	2	10	1	2	—	5	2	25	8.33
Total	**25**	**25**	**25**	**25**	**25**	**25**	**25**	**25**	**25**	**25**	**25**	**25**	**300**	**100.00**

(Contd.)

	Janmabhoomi programme													
Yes	24	25	25	25	25	25	24	25	25	25	25	25	298	99.33
No	1	—	—	—	—	—	1	—	—	—	—	—	2	0.67
Total	**25**	**25**	**25**	**25**	**25**	**25**	**25**	**25**	**25**	**25**	**25**	**25**	**300**	**100.00**
	AIDS awareness programmme													
Yes	23	25	21	24	15	21	13	15	15	22	17	15	226	75.33
No	2	—	4	1	10	4	12	10	10	3	8	10	74	24.67
Total	**25**	**25**	**25**	**25**	**25**	**25**	**25**	**25**	**25**	**25**	**25**	**25**	**300**	**100.00**
	Any other specify													
Yes	1	1	—	2	—	—	—	1	—	—	—	—	5	1.67
No	24	25	25	23	25	25	25	24	25	25	25	25	295	98.33
Total	**25**	**25**	**25**	**25**	**25**	**25**	**25**	**25**	**25**	**25**	**25**	**25**	**300**	**100.00**

Table—4.51. Distribution of the respondents according to their benefit by Janmabhoomi programme

Benefit	*TRD*				*CRD*				*MRD*				*Total*	*Percen-tage (%)*
	RGM	*SKM*	*PKM*	*VPM*	*CTM*	*VDM*	*NVM*	*IRM*	*CGM*	*MPM*	*KVM*	*KPM*		
Yes	23	24	23	25	25	25	24	24	25	25	25	24	292	97.33
No	2	1	2	—	—	—	1	1	—	—	—	1	8	2.67
Total	**25**	**25**	**25**	**25**	**25**	**25**	**25**	**25**	**25**	**25**	**25**	**25**	**300**	**100.00**

Table—4.52. Distribution of the respondents according to their rank order benefitted by Janmabhoomi programme

Rank	*TRD*				*CRD*				*MRD*				*Total*	*Percen-tage (%)*
	RGM	*SKM*	*PKM*	*VPM*	*CTM*	*VDM*	*NVM*	*IRM*	*CGM*	*MPM*	*KVM*	*KPM*		
High	18	19	19	22	21	21	13	22	22	20	19	9	225	75
Medium	7	6	6	3	4	4	12	3	3	5	6	16	75	25
Low	—	—	—	—	—	—	—	—	—	—	—	—	—	—
Total	**25**	**25**	**25**	**25**	**25**	**25**	**25**	**25**	**25**	**25**	**25**	**25**	**300**	**100.00**

Table-4.51 shows distribution of the respondents according to their benefit by Janmabhoomi Programme. According to the data, 292 respondents (97.33 per cent) told that they are benefitted by Janmabhoomi Programme and 8 respondents (2.67 per cent) told that they are not benefitted by Janmabhoomi Programme.

Table-4.52 shows distribution of the respondents according to their rank order benefitted by Janmabhoomi programme. According to the data, 225 respondents (75 per cent) told that they are highly benefitted by Janmabhoomi programme followed by 75 respondents (25 per cent) told that they are moderately benefitted by Janmabhoomi programme.

Table-4.53 shows distribution of the respondents according to their opinion on Mahila Janmabhoomi programme. According to the data, 278 respondents (92.67 per cent) expressed that Mahila Janmabhoomi programme was good and useful programme followed by 21 respondents (7 per cent) opined that it was moderate and only one respondent (0.33 per cent) opined it was low not that much of useful.

Table-4.54 shows respondents membership in various committee's. According to the data, 279 respondents (93 per cent) are members in Mother's committee's, followed by 258 respondents (86 per cent) are members in Educational committee's, 267 respondents (89 per cent) are members in the committee's on Violence against women, 298 respondents (99.33 per cent) are members in Vanasamrakshana samithi, 10 respondents (3.33 per cent) are in Water shed committees, 12 respondents (4 per cent) are members in Water users committees.

Table-4.55 shows distribution of the respondents according to the govt/voluntary agencies taking steps to help SHGs. According to the data, 299 respondents (99.67 per cent) told that the govt/voluntary agencies are taking steps to help SHGs. But only one respondent (0.33 per cent) told that the govt/voluntary agencies are not taking any steps to help SHGs.

Table—4.53. Distribution of the respondents according to their opinion on Mahila Janmabhoomi programme

Opinion	*TRD*				*CRD*				*MRD*				*Total*	*Percen-tage (%)*
	RGM	*SKM*	*PKM*	*VPM*	*CTM*	*VDM*	*NVM*	*IRM*	*CGM*	*MPM*	*KVM*	*KPM*		
Good	19	25	23	24	25	24	24	24	25	23	23	19	278	92.67
Moderate	6	—	1	1	—	1	1	—	—	2	2	6	21	7.00
Low	—	—	1	—	—	—	—	—	—	—	—	—	1	0.33
Total	25	25	25	25	25	25	25	25	25	25	25	25	300	100.00

Table—4.54. Distribution of the respondents according to their membership in Various committees

Committee's	*TRD*				*CRD*				*MRD*				*Total*	*Percentage (%)*
	RGM	*SKM*	*PKM*	*VPM*	*CTM*	*VDM*	*NVM*	*IRM*	*CGM*	*MPM*	*KVM*	*KPM*		
Mother's committee														
Yes	2	4	1	2	1	4	4	—	1	1	—	1	21	7.00
No	23	21	24	23	24	21	21	25	24	24	25	24	279	93.00
Total	**25**	**25**	**25**	**25**	**25**	**25**	**25**	**25**	**25**	**25**	**25**	**25**	**300**	**100.00**
Educational committee participation														
Yes	8	2	1	1	3	7	3	4	6	4	1	2	42	14.00
No	17	23	24	24	22	18	22	21	19	21	24	23	258	86.00
Total	**25**	**25**	**25**	**25**	**25**	**25**	**25**	**25**	**25**	**25**	**25**	**25**	**300**	**100.00**
Committee on violence against women														
Yes	4	—	—	—	4	4	8	6	4	—	—	3	33	11.00
No	21	25	25	25	21	21	17	19	21	25	25	22	267	89.00
Total	**25**	**25**	**25**	**25**	**25**	**25**	**25**	**25**	**25**	**25**	**25**	**25**	**300**	**100.00**

(Contd.)

Vana samrakshana samithi														
Yes	—	1	—	—	—	—	1	—	—	—	—	—	2	0.67
No	25	24	25	25	25	25	24	25	25	25	25	25	298	99.33
Total	**25**	**25**	**25**	**25**	**25**	**25**	**25**	**25**	**25**	**25**	**25**	**25**	**300**	**100.00**
Water shed committee														
Yes	1	—	—	—	—	—	2	—	3	—	3	1	10	3.33
No	24	25	25	25	25	25	23	25	22	25	22	24	290	96.67
Total	**25**	**25**	**25**	**25**	**25**	**25**	**25**	**25**	**25**	**25**	**25**	**25**	**300**	**100.00**
Water users														
Yes	2	1	—	—	—	3	1	1	1	—	—	3	12	4.00
No	23	24	25	25	25	22	24	24	24	25	25	22	288	96.00
Total	**25**	**25**	**25**	**25**	**25**	**25**	**25**	**25**	**25**	**25**	**25**	**25**	**300**	**100.00**

Table—4.55. Distribution of the respondents according to their opinion on government/voluntary agencies taking steps to help SHGs

Steps	*TRD*				*CRD*				*MRD*				*Total*	*Percentage (%)*
	RGM	*SKM*	*PKM*	*VPM*	*CTM*	*VDM*	*NVM*	*IRM*	*CGM*	*MPM*	*KVM*	*KPM*		
Yes	25	25	25	25	25	25	25	25	25	25	24	25	299	99.67
No	—	—	—	—	—	—	—	—	—	—	1	—	1	0.33
Total	**25**	**25**	**25**	**25**	**25**	**25**	**25**	**25**	**25**	**25**	**25**	**25**	**300**	**100.00**

Table—4.56. Distribution of the respondents according to the essential characteristics for running SHG

Opinion	*TRD*				*CRD*				*MRD*				*Total*	*Percen-tage (%)*
	RGM	*SKM*	*PKM*	*VPM*	*CTM*	*VDM*	*NVM*	*IRM*	*CGM*	*MPM*	*KVM*	*KPM*		
Appropriate skill/training	3	—	—	—	—	2	—	—	—	—	—	—	5	1.67
Courage	5	1	—	—	—	5	—	—	—	—	—	—	11	3.66
Self confidence	2	—	—	—	—	1	—	—	—	—	—	—	3	1.00
Sincerity in savings and meetings	8	11	10	5	14	11	15	10	15	11	11	6	127	42.33
Co-operation	2	10	7	6	11	1	10	15	7	6	13	10	98	32.67
All the above	5	3	8	14	—	5	—	—	3	8	1	9	56	18.67
Total	**25**	**25**	**25**	**25**	**25**	**25**	**25**	**25**	**25**	**25**	**25**	**25**	**300**	**100.00**

Table-4.56 shows respondents opinion on the essential characteristics for running SHGs and secret of success. According to the data, 127 respondents (42.33 per cent) opined sincerity in savings and meetings followed by 98 respondents (32.67 per cent) expressed co-operation, elevan respondents (3.67 per cent) expressed courage and 56 respondents (18.67 per cent) expressed all the above characteristics are essential for running SHGs.

Table-4.57 shows distribution of the respondents according to their family members help in respondents work in addition to their efforts. According to the data, 229 respondents (76.33 per cent) told that their husbands help in respondents work followed by 22 respondents (7.33 per cent) told that all members of their family helps their work and 20 respondents (6.67 per cent) told that nobody can not help in their work. The rest of them told that their parents, in-laws and children help in respondents works in addition to their efforts.

Table-4.58 shows distribution of the respondents according to their attitude of the respondents family members joining in SHGs. According to the data, 242 respondents (80.67 per cent) have strong support from their family members, 54 respondents (18 per cent) have moderate support and only four respondents (1.33 per cent) have no support from their family members.

Table-4.59 shows distribution of the respondents according to their parents/husbands present attitude towards SHG women. According to the data, 178 respondents (59.33 per cent) told that their parents/husbands present attitude towards SHG is most co-operative, 120 respondents (40 per cent) told that their parents/husbands present attitude is somewhat co-operative and the rest of them told that their parents/husbands present attitude is indifferent.

Table-4.60 shows the health problems of the respondents. Majority of the respondents (75 per cent) have no health problems. According to the data, 60 respondents (20 per cent) have general health problems followed by five respondents (1.67 per cent) suffer from asthma and seven respondents (2.33 per cent) are physically handicapped. Rest of the respondents suffer from cancer and heart problems.

Table—4.57. Distribution of the respondents according to their family members help in respondents work

Family members	*TRD*				*CRD*				*MRD*				*Total*	*Percentage (%)*
	RGM	*SKM*	*PKM*	*VPM*	*CTM*	*VDM*	*NVM*	*IRM*	*CGM*	*MPM*	*KVM*	*KPM*		
Parents	—	—	—	1	1	2	1	—	—	1	—	—	6	2.00
Husband	17	21	12	23	21	18	20	19	15	20	22	21	229	76.33
In-Laws	1	—	1	—	—	—	—	1	1	—	1	—	5	1.67
Children	2	1	4	1	1	2	—	1	1	1	1	3	18	6.00
All members	4	2	1	—	1	3	2	1	7	1	—	—	22	7.33
No body	1	1	7	—	1	—	2	3	1	2	1	1	20	6.67
Total	**25**	**25**	**25**	**25**	**25**	**25**	**25**	**25**	**25**	**25**	**25**	**25**	**300**	**100.00**

Table—4.58. Distribution of the respondents according to the attitude of the family members joining in SHGs

Attitude	*TRD*				*CRD*				*MRD*				*Total*	*Percentage (%)*
	RGM	*SKM*	*PKM*	*VPM*	*CTM*	*VDM*	*NVM*	*IRM*	*CGM*	*MPM*	*KVM*	*KPM*		
Strong support	16	20	24	20	24	17	23	24	15	24	14	21	242	80.67
Moderate support	8	5	1	5	1	7	2	1	9	1	10	4	54	18.00
Indifferent	1	—	—	—	—	1	—	—	1	—	1	—	4	1.33
Total	**25**	**25**	**25**	**25**	**25**	**25**	**25**	**25**	**25**	**25**	**25**	**25**	**300**	**100.00**

Table—4.59. Distribution of the respondents according to their parents/husbands present attitude towards SHG women

Attitude of parents/ husbands	*TRD*				*CRD*				*MRD*				*Total*	*Percentage (%)*
	RGM	*SKM*	*PKM*	*VPM*	*CTM*	*VDM*	*NVM*	*IRM*	*CGM*	*MPM*	*KVM*	*KPM*		
Most co-operative	12	15	14	18	19	14	21	19	11	15	9	11	178	59.33
Somewhat co-operative	13	10	11	7	6	11	4	6	12	10	16	14	120	40.00
Indifferent	—	—	—	—	—	—	—	—	2	—	—	—	2	0.67
Total	**25**	**25**	**25**	**25**	**25**	**25**	**25**	**25**	**25**	**25**	**25**	**25**	**300**	**100.00**

Table—4.60. Distribution of the respondents according to their health problems

Health problems	*TRD*				*CRD*				*MRD*				*Total*	*Percentage (%)*
	RGM	*SKM*	*PKM*	*VPM*	*CTM*	*VDM*	*NVM*	*IRM*	*CGM*	*MPM*	*KVM*	*KPM*		
No Problem	14	12	23	19	22	18	17	21	21	17	19	22	225	75.00
General health problems	10	12	2	5	1	7	6	2	2	6	4	3	60	20.00
Physically handicapped	—	1	—	—	1	—	2	1	2	—	—	—	7	2.33
Asthma	1	—	—	—	1	—	—	—	—	1	2	—	5	1.67
Cancer	—	—	—	—	—	—	—	1	—	—	—	—	1	0.33
Heart problem	—	—	—	1	—	—	—	—	—	1	—	—	2	0.67
Total	**25**	**25**	**25**	**25**	**25**	**25**	**25**	**25**	**25**	**25**	**25**	**25**	**300**	**100.00**

Table—4.61. Distribution of the respondents according to receiving of gas connection

Gas connection	*TRD*				*CRD*				*MRD*				*Total*	*Percentage (%)*
	RGM	*SKM*	*PKM*	*VPM*	*CTM*	*VDM*	*NVM*	*IRM*	*CGM*	*MPM*	*KVM*	*KPM*		
Yes	17	16	18	11	13	15	2	14	17	14	7	12	156	52.00
No	8	9	7	14	12	10	23	11	8	11	18	13	144	48.00
Total	**25**	**25**	**25**	**25**	**25**	**25**	**25**	**25**	**25**	**25**	**25**	**25**	**300**	**100.00**

Table-4.61 shows distribution of the respondents according to receiving of gas connection. According to the data, 156 respondents (52 per cent) received gas connections and 144 respondents (48 per cent) have not received any gas connection.

Table-4.62 shows distribution of the respondents according to the category of self-employment that women are engaged in sequel to empowerment in SHGs. According to the data, 87 respondents (29 per cent) are engaged in curry powders/papads/eatable items followed by 59 respondents (19.67 per cent) engaged in dairying, 49 respondents (16.33 per cent) engaged in business, 44 respondents (14.67 per cent) engaged in sheep, goat and cattle rearing, 30 respondents (10 per cent) engaged in idli, dosa stals. The rest of the respondents are engaged in cultivation, Gonisanchi tayaree/tailoring, Ragichembula tayaree and traditional occupation.

Table-4.63 shows distribution of the respondents according to the difficulty in selling out the products. According to the data, 257 respondents (85.67 per cent) told that there is no difficulty in selling out the products and 43 respondents (14.33 per cent) told that there is difficulty in selling out the products.

Table-4.64 shows distribution of the respondents according to their rate in present venture. According to the data, 234 respondents (78 per cent) told that they are moderate in present venture followed by 59 respondents (19.67 per cent) told that they are successful and seven respondents (2.33 per cent) are at loss in present venture.

The data in Table-4.65 shows respondents have no idea in starting another SHG in addition to the existing one. According to the data, two respondents (0.67 per cent) in Renigunta Mandal told that they have an idea to start another SHG in addition to the existing one and 298 respondents (99.33 per cent) told that they have no idea to start another SHG in addition to the existing one.

Table—4.62. Distribution of the respondents according to the category of self-employment

Self employ-ment	*TRD*				*CRD*				*MRD*				*Total*	*Percen-tage (%)*
	RGM	*SKM*	*PKM*	*VPM*	*CTM*	*VDM*	*NVM*	*IRM*	*CGM*	*MPM*	*KVM*	*KPM*		
Dairying	6	10	3	6	7	5	—	8	5	2	3	4	59	19.67
Cultivation	—	4	—	—	—	—	2	—	2	2	—	1	11	3.67
Idli/Dosa stalls	—	—	7	1	5	1	5	4	2	2	1	2	30	10.00
Business	3	1	4	3	2	2	4	3	10	9	2	6	49	16.33
Sheep, Goat and Cattle rearing	9	6	3	4	9	6	—	6	—	1	—	—	44	14.67
Gonisanchi Tayaree/ Tailoring	1	—	—	—	—	3	1	—	—	1	—	—	6	2.00
Ragichembula Tayaree	2	1	—	—	—	1	—	—	—	2	—	1	7	2.33
Curry powders/ Papads/ eatable items	4	3	8	11	2	7	10	3	6	4	19	11	87	29.00

(Contd.)

Traditional occupation	—	—	—	—	—	—	3	1	—	2	—	—	6	2.00
Total	**25**	**25**	**25**	**25**	**25**	**25**	**25**	**25**	**25**	**25**	**25**	**25**	**300**	**100.00**

Table—4.63. Distribution of the respondents according to the difficulty in selling out the goods

Difficulty	*TRD*				*CRD*				*MRD*				*Total*	*Percentage (%)*
	RGM	*SKM*	*PKM*	*VPM*	*CTM*	*VDM*	*NVM*	*IRM*	*CGM*	*MPM*	*KVM*	*KPM*		
Yes	4	—	—	—	8	8	6	6	4	—	2	5	43	14.33
No	21	25	25	25	17	17	19	19	21	25	23	20	257	85.67
Total	**25**	**25**	**25**	**25**	**25**	**25**	**25**	**25**	**25**	**25**	**25**	**25**	**300**	**100.00**

Table—4.64. Distribution of the respondents according to their rate in present venture

Rate	*TRD*				*CRD*				*MRD*				*Total*	*Percen-tage (%)*
	RGM	*SKM*	*PKM*	*VPM*	*CTM*	*VDM*	*NVM*	*IRM*	*CGM*	*MPM*	*KVM*	*KPM*		
Successful	1	5	6	2	11	4	3	8	4	12	2	1	59	19.67
Moderate	23	18	19	23	14	20	22	17	19	13	23	23	234	78.00
Loss	1	2	—	—	—	1	—	—	—	—	—	1	7	2.33
Total	**25**	**25**	**25**	**25**	**25**	**25**	**25**	**25**	**25**	**25**	**25**	**25**	**300**	**100.00**

Table—4.65. Distribution of the respondents according to their idea to start another SHG

Idea	*TRD*				*CRD*				*MRD*				*Total*	*Percen-tage (%)*
	RGM	*SKM*	*PKM*	*VPM*	*CTM*	*VDM*	*NVM*	*IRM*	*CGM*	*MPM*	*KVM*	*KPM*		
Yes	2	—	—	—	—	—	—	—	—	—	—	—	2	0.67
No	23	25	25	25	25	25	25	25	25	25	25	25	298	99.33
Total	**25**	**25**	**25**	**25**	**25**	**25**	**25**	**25**	**25**	**25**	**25**	**25**	**300**	**100.00**

Table—4.66. Distribution of the respondents according to their satisfaction after joining the group

Satisfaction	*TRD*				*CRD*				*MRD*				*Total*	*Percentage (%)*
	RGM	*SKM*	*PKM*	*VPM*	*CTM*	*VDM*	*NVM*	*IRM*	*CGM*	*MPM*	*KVM*	*KPM*		
Yes	21	21	23	23	23	20	25	22	24	22	23	22	269	89.67
No	4	4	2	2	2	5	—	3	1	3	2	3	31	10.33
Total	**25**	**25**	**25**	**25**	**25**	**25**	**25**	**25**	**25**	**25**	**25**	**25**	**300**	**100.00**

Table-4.66 shows distribution of the respondents according to their satisfaction after joining in the SHG group. According to the data, 269 respondents (89.67 per cent) expressed that they are satisfied after joining in the group. The rest of them are not satisfied with internal differences, non co-operation of the members and leaders.

Table-4.67 shows distribution of the respondents suggestions to improve the programme. According to the data, 174 respondents (58.00 per cent) expressed that subsidy on loans have to be sanctioned in order to improve the programme, followed by 74 respondents (24.67 per cent) expressed that to provide technical training to take up self employment and 41 respondents (13.67 per cent) expressed to provide training programmes. Rest of them expressed to arrange orientation programmes to all SHG women.

Table—4.67. Distribution of the respondents according to their suggestions to improve the programme

Sugges-tions	*TRD*				*CRD*				*MRD*				*Total*	*Percen-tage (%)*
	RGM	*SKM*	*PKM*	*VPM*	*CTM*	*VDM*	*NVM*	*IRM*	*CGM*	*MPM*	*KVM*	*KPM*		
To sanction subsidy on loans	6	10	17	20	21	7	17	20	13	17	13	13	174	58.00
To provide technical training to take up self employment	5	8	8	4	2	1	7	2	12	5	8	12	74	24.67
To provide training programmes	12	3	—	—	2	17	1	3	—	—	3	—	41	13.67
To provide orientation programmes	2	4	—	1	—	—	—	—	—	3	1	—	11	3.67
Total	**25**	**25**	**25**	**25**	**25**	**25**	**25**	**25**	**25**	**25**	**25**	**25**	**300**	**100.00**

5

SUMMARY AND CONCLUSION

A total of 300 women leaders and members of SHG groups were interviewed for the study by adopting an interview schedule. The interviews took place in the local language *i.e.,* Telugu. The interviewer also took the opportunity of observing the functioning of SHG by being a non-participant observer in the sittings of some of the SHG groups during the period of field work.

Major Findings of the Study

— The sample were drawn from different age groups, both young and middle aged : 3(1%) of them are aged below 20 years, 95 (31.67%) between 20 and 30 years, 123 (41%) between 30 and 40 years, 54 (18%) between 40 and 50 years, 24 (8%) between 50 and 60 years and only 1 (0.33%) above 60 years (see Table-1). The fact that almost the total sample was young or middle-aged should be viewed in the background of propagation and encouragement of SHG groups only for last six to seven years in the state.

— Socio-economic background : The respondents hailed from different castes and levels : 62 (20.67%) from upper caste background, 150 (50%) from backward castes 76 (25.33%) from scheduled castes and 12 (4%) from scheduled tribes (see Table-3). As the SHG groups are encouraged among sections which are below the poverty line (BPL) and as most of the poor hail from BC, SC and ST sections. There are 11(3.67%) Muslim respondents and the rest of them are Hindus.

— Most of the respondents (N 53 ; 17.67%) are illiterates. 28 respondents (9.33%) are literates, 30 (10%) have lower primary, 37 (12.33%) have primary, 76 (25.33%) have upper primary, 53 (17.67%) have high school education, 18 (6%) are intermediate, 2 (0.67%) have degree qualification and 3 (1%) have technical education (see Table-5).

— The income of the respondents is also mostly moderate. The distribution of the respondents among various income groups reveals that most of the respondents *i.e.* 248 (82%) of them had an income of over Rs. 1000 but below Rs. 10,000.50 (16.67%) are earned below Rs. 1000 and only 2 (0.67%) had an income of over Rs. 10,000 (see Table-13). Still, it can be deduced that those with meagre incomes are unable to join SHG groups as they may find it difficult to save even Rs. 30 per month.

— As the sample is based in villages, most of them (N 112; 37.33%) hailed from coolies. Some of them (N 41; 13.67%) lived by cultivating the land taken on lease, some (N 50; 16.67%) have dairying, some (No. 31; 10.33%) sustained by business and others (N 66; 22%) by other occupations (See Table-10). It is heartening to note that a majority of the sample, although to note that a majority of the sample, although illiterate and from agrarian labour background had chosen to join SHG groups.

— The selected sample are members of 300 different SHG groups and 119 (39.67%) of them are motivated by neighbours and only 13 groups had a membership of 10 and that of the others ranged between 10 and 15.

— The amount saved by the largest respondents ranged from Rs. 30 to Rs. 40. Some of the respondents 139 (46.33%) saved from Rs. 50 and above, only one of the respondent saved the amount ranged from Rs. 40 to Rs. 50.

Most of the respondents took the loans from the group fund. The main purpose of taken these loans are 56 (18.67%) took the loan to start dairy, 48 (16%) took the loan for the domestic purpose, 54 (18%) are for the purpose of business, 37 (12.33%) are sheep/goat/cattle rearing. Rest of them have taken loan for the purpose of cultivation, petty shop, Ragichembulu tayaree, Tailoring etc. 59 (19.67%) of the respondents have not utilised the purpose of taking loans.

The above reflects a marked change in the perceived status of women. Frequent meetings of women as routine exercises of self help groups enable them, besides settling the business matters, to interact and communicate with each other and share their problems and suggest solutions which tend to boost their confidence. This, in turn, will have manifest and latent consequences on the inter-personal relations both in the family and community.

Impact of SHGs on Empowerment of Women

All the members of the groups are asked to state the changes and improvements they have achieved as a result of their association with SHG. Most of them appreciated and acknowledged the all round benefits of SHG.

The Achievements are as Follows :

- Economic empowerment and improvement in economic status.
- Social mobility increased through exposure to outside world.
- Developed team spirit and became organized group of employment.

- Nutritional and health status improved through greater awareness and better utilization of health services.
- Improved the sanitary conditions because of the construction of individual latrines.
- Awareness on small family norm and adoption of family planning increased.
- Interaction with government officials and started questioning the government agencies to get their rights.
- Habit of newspaper reading and watching T.V. increased to get more information about day-to-day affairs and government programmes and policies.
- In the family decision making capacities increased and fairly attained equality in family matters.
- A large majority of the respondents (N. 292; 97.33%) stated that they are able to take independent decisions on various family matters and also implemented them (see Table-16).
- Over all positive changes in the life styles such as proper food habits, education of children, dress pattern, beauty conscious, acquisition of modern gadgets, personal hygiene and so on enhanced.
- Awareness on age at marriage increased.
- Social mobility and free movements within and outside village increased.

On the whole a higher level of empowerment on several facts of life manifested no longer the traditional, timid, submissive and oppressive behaviour. Since they play a major supportive role in the family through their economic support to the family most of their husbands have appreciated their activities and in fact they support and encourage them.

Problems

Favouritism problems arise when the group leader has to decide about the lending. If the leader shows any favouritism to the persons close to the leader then certain problems crop up.

Marketing

Majority of the members will have to depend on the local markets as the major possibility of exhibiting their products. Only a few groups who have contact with state level officers, will be getting the opportunity of exhibiting the products at state/national level. Therefore majority of them are defined of the benefit of sales. Besides some of the products, due to the poor quality are not able to compete with commercial goods in the global market.

Delays in government procedures in sanctioning the loans affected their work. Majority of the groups are running without any financial assistance from the government. Hence they are not able to start any income generation activities with more investment.

Group Rivalry

Most of the groups are dominated by some active leaders and high caste people. Sometimes even young girls, who are educated and aware of things may dominate other members. Sometimes poor illiterate members are exploited by the active members.

Obstacles for the Sustainability of SHGs

The following are some of the obstacles for the sustainability of self help groups :

- Irregular groups meetings.
- Irregularity in savings.
- Lump sum contribution in the form of savings to attain eligibility for higher loans.
- Loans to members only on entitlement (Pro-rata) basis without reference to nature of need.

- Large loans only to few members.
- Absence of proper and up-to-date record keeping.
- Absence of regular system of weekly/monthly repayment of loans by the members to SHGs.
- Lack of confidence among bank branches to extend loans to SHGs in the absence of NGO's.
- Lack of proper understanding and internalisation of SHGs concepts among banks and governmental agencies.
- Insistence by bank branches for blocking entire cash savings of SHGs with them.
- Insistence on collaterals by banks for extending loans to SHGs.
- Repayment of bank loan instalments by raising loans from other sources.
- Absence of rotation in leadership positions.

Strategies for the Sustainability of SHGs

The following are some of the strategies to ensure sustainability of SHGs

- Group is a compact and members by and large exhibit homogeneity in social and/or economic context conforming to eligibility criteria.
- High level of motivation of members and group has internalised the essential concepts of self help and mutual help as building blocks of the group.
- Effective participation of all members and decisions are taken democratically on consensual basis after indepth discussions in the group meetings.
- Evolve and introduce appropriate savings products for regular and special savings and regular savings are used for internal lending for consumption and/or production needs.
- Group is able to screen the loan requests and approves loans based on the individual needs.
- Collateral consists of mutual confidence and trust.

- Decide upon appropriate market related interest rate and facilitate the process of internal capitalisation.
- Enforces repayment of loans through peer pressure and group dynamics.
- Ability to scan environment for diversifying their activities with a view to increasing income levels with or without the support of extension agents/ social animators.
- Ability to access required non-financial services.
- Participate in social issues of mutual interests like literacy, health care and family planning, immunisation, enrolment of children in schools participation in community works and others.
- Records and accounts maintenance is upto date and good.
- Strength of SHGs is reflected in group cohesion and vibrant behaviour.
- Fungibility of savings and credit cycles in SHG help consolidate the group behaviour.
- SHG inculcate thrift habits and increase in level of savings among rural poor.
- Improvement in access to credit.
- Financing of unique and non-traditional activities.
- Definite shift in loaning pattern from consumption to productive activities.
- Improvement in loan volumes of SHGs through internal capitalisation.
- Quality of loan appraisal and supervision improved with increase in loan portfolios.
- Almost cent-percent recovery of loans at SHG level interest rates at group level are ajusted to market conditions.

- Greater awareness of the need to higher economic operations.
- Creation of common and community assets.
- Reduction in transaction cost of banks and borrower alike.
- Simplified loaning procedure and documentation.
- Excellent recovery performance of loans extended to SHGs
- SHGs help banks to expand good clientele base among rural poor.
- SHGs provide favourable climate for conscious leadership development, decentralised decision-making, peer pressure and sustainability of group action.
- Participation in socio-economic development programmes like literacy, health, nutrition, housing, primary education, sanitation etc., by matured SHGs have contributed to overall empowerment and sustainability of rural poor.
- The scheduled castes, the scheduled tribes, backward class and minority women are estimated to contribute 80 per cent of social labour to strengthen the national economy. In the words of Katti Padma Rao, an active propagandist of dalit ideology, dalit women is a social force, leading a life full of confusion and conflict.

In this regard steps should be taken to alleviate the status of dalit women, who are the poorest of the poorer sections by concentrating more on literacy. The Dubagunta Anti-alcoholic Movement is a clear outcome of adult literacy programme. In the same way, the sustainability of SHG movement and its further development depends more on how far women are aware of their plight and to avail the opportunities targeted for their benefit. Hence, stress should be more on adult literacy missions, besides primary education.

- Just like in the agricultural sector, support price should be fixed to their products, if not it is not competent for them to compete in the open market.
- The New Economic Order has been adversely affecting women and they are becoming poorer, with the increasing rate of marginality among women workers. The reasons for increasing marginality of women workers is that firstly, they are entering the market without skills. Secondly, the patriarchal system is obstructing them in availing the skills. In this regard, steps should be taken to impart vocational training to women workers in order to reap the opportunities developing from the new economic structure in addition to literacy and education. For this, the institution of family should also play a dynamic role, while breaking the shackles of patriarchy and supporting their women members productively.

Suggestions for the Improvement of SHGs

The following suggestions are made for the improvement of SHGs.

- Continuing education programme can be conducted for illiterate members.
- The members may be given training on managerial and leadership skills and may be motivated to present themselves in panchayat elections and to take part in the political activities.
- The SHG members may be motivated to prepare annual action plans in their group which will be useful in planning their activities efficiently.
- Emphasis must be focused in various programmes to change the patriarchal system which still control and keep the women away from involvement and decision making.

- The members must be motivated to involve legislation in developmental activities for the betterment of their community.
- One important thing to be kept in mind while forming self help group for any specific programme are intriguing question about to be raised is the degree to which it/they can be replicated or scaled up.

Case Studies

The following case studies highlight the socio-economic conditions of the respondents. They also show the efforts made by the respondents in taking up various income generation programmes through SHGs and their opinions about the scheme have also been mentioned.

Reasons Behind the Success

The Chittoor district has a number of success stories. Basically, the collector is very active, he personally meets the SHG/DWCRA groups and women and encourages them to strengthen their groups. He also encourages them to become literate and arrange care for their children. As a result most of the women got self confidence, able to express themselves, questioning the government authorities if any irregularities are committed on their group. SHG leaders are also members of the education committees of most of the schools. They question the teachers, if they are irregular.

SHG members are able to deal with problem of family and husband, they are able to participate in decision making which we rarely see even in urban, educated and working women. They are able to question their husbands and solve the problems. They have realized and bad impact of caste system, now members belonging to all the castes mingle freely, meet together, share the experiences and work together. Such universal cooperation helps their productive work on a sustained manner.

Case Study-1

What a Pride ?

"For the first time my husband asked me" Lakshmi We have to purchase manures to the crop. Can you bring Rs. 1,000 loan from your Podupulakshmi ? I will give it back to you after harvesting". I am very happy now. Podupulakshmi has not only given me thousand rupees loan but also something more that increases the value of my life.

Smt. Varalakshmi, Panabakam

Case Study-2

Change in Attitude !!

"I used to be a lazy women. I used to go to work once or twice in a week. My Husband and in-law's are angry with me for my laziness. I never cared them. Recently I joined in Podupulaksmi along with my friends. My Husband refused to give me money. He told me that "you earn money by yourself" I couldn't pay my daily contribution to my group leader. All my friends are regular payers of Podupulakshmi. How can I stop saving half way. All may look me down. So-Now I am going to work every day. Otherwise How can I save one rupee"?

Smt. Jayamma, Kayampeta

Case Study-3

A Wise Decision

"I thought it is very difficult for me to save one rupee per day. My grand mother advised me to keep away a handful of rice every day. What a Surprise! I am able to save three kgs of rice per month that means Rs. 20.00. Now I am confident that I can also save the other 10 rupees".

Smt. Beezan, Molakalacheruvu

Case Study-4

Chocolate or Saving Money ?

"My five year old son is very naughty and mischievous. He always used to harass me by asking me" Ma! give me one rupee I have to buy Chocolate". Now-a-days I am taking him to the Podupulakshmi group meetings also with me. Yesterday my son asked me "Ma! give me one rupee I have to join in Podupulakshmi" I love not only my son but also Podupulakshmi. *Smt. Ademma, Peruru*

Case Study-5

One Rupee—A Life Saving drug

"I was having uterus problem for a long time but I could not pay for the treatment. 'Podupulakshmi' has given me Rs. 1000/- loan. I got operated in time. Now I am healthy. I saved one rupee per day and it saved my life".

Smt. Seshamma, Penuballi, Nimmaluru

Case Study-6

A thought for the last day

"I am a old lady of 60 years. The other younger women of my group used to tease me. They said" Grand Ma! "why and for whom you are saving one rupee per day in this age"? I told them I never saved anything in my life. At least this money may be useful for my funeral. Late better than never what do you say? *Smt. Begum, Gajulamandyam*

Case Study-7

An expression of a self confident woman!

"Two years before I was alone. Now we are five hundred women in Podupulakshmi groups of our village. Two years before I started saving one rupee. Today I am one of the partners of 4 Lakh rupees village fund in Aplayagunta".

Smt. Rama Devi, Aplayagunta

Case Study-8

Guramma is 43 years old. She belongs to backward community. She studied only upto 3rd standard as her parents are economically poor. She was married at the age of 15 years and her husband is a labourer. Her marriage was arranged by her parents. Her family is a nuclear family. She has one daughter and one son. Two of them are married.

She joined in self help group in 1996 and the group is Sravani. She was a labourer before joining SHG. Both of their earnings were not sufficient for their family. They were in debts. With the intention of supplementing her house hold's income, she joined in self help group. At the beginning, she was not that much interested and satisfied. Later on with the motivation by her neighbours, she came to know the uses of the amount and how to utilise the amount. Now she earns by making leaf plates assisted by her husband and is able to get expected results.

Smt. Guramma, Anupalli

Case Study-9

Nagarathnamma is 40 years old and belongs to backward community. She is a literate women. She got married at the age of 15 years. It was an arranged marriage. She has two sisters and two brothers. She is the second child in her family. After marriage all of them lived together for 3 years. After that they were separated from her family along with her husband. She has a daughter and son. Her daughter has studied 5th standard and is married. She joined in self help group in the year 1997 and the group is Sri Balaji. She is the leader of the group.

Nagarathnamma earns Rs. 600/- to Rs. 700/- per month from milk business. She got a loan of Rs. 4000/- to buy a cow where as the cow costs Rs. 8000/-. The loan should be repaid with in one and half year. She sells the milk to improve financial position. She feels that the SHG programme has helped her to have a better livelihood.

Smt. Nagarathnamma, Kadiri

Case Study-10

Parvathamma got married to Krishna Murthy at the age of 18 years. She belongs to forward community. She has one daughter and one son. Son studying 10th standard. Her husband was a business man. But unfortunately he got heart attack and died.

Now she is living alone and no one of her sons came forward to look after her. She has one pucca/own house which was given to her when her husband was alive. Now she is 37 years old. In this situation their neighbours and relatives motivated her to join in self help group.

Then she joined in SHG and her savings in group is Rs. 30/- per month. She got revolving fund Rs. 1000/- and with that money she started tailoring. In 1995 they formed a group. In 1996 they got revolving fund. She has performed marriage of her daughter. Now her livelihood has totally changed and the family members are living happily. Before joining she used to work hard for getting food to all her family members.

Smt. Parvathamma, Chinnagottigallu

Case Study-11

Swarnalatha is 45 years old and belongs to backward community. She stopped her education at 7th standard. She got married at the age of 18 years. Her marriage was arranged by her parents. She has two daughters and one of them is studying in the college and the second one is doing technical work in BSSK. Her husband is a private employee.

She joined in SHG in the year 1998 and the group is Sravani. Leaf plate making is her primary occupation. She was not doing any business before joining SHG programme. At the beginning, she was saving Rs. 40/- per month. Now she is saving Rs. 50/- per month.

She feels that her position is economically improved but she also feels that it is risky too. She has to spend more towards auto charges. She is interested in money saving and feels joining in SHG gives her that opportunity.

Smt. Swarnalatha, Renigunta

Case Study-12

Nagamma is 40 years old. At the age of 17 years she got married with Venkatramana. She has one son and three daughters. Her husband was adicted to alcohol and used to have alcohol daily and due to this his liver was spoiled. After some time he died. They had no other financial assistance. Only way for her livelihood is from daily wage work. After the death of her husband it became very difficult for her to maintain the family.

After some time she is motivated by Mandal Development Officer and joined in SHG group. Her SHG name is Lakshmi Saraswathi group. They joined the group in 1996. In 1997 they received revolving fund of Rs. 10,000/-. Then whole group started super bazaar with that money and every member is involved in maintaining the super bazaar. In 1998 they got two times revolving fund of Rs. 10,000/- and Rs. 9,000/-. For her first daughters marriage the SHG group members helped Rs. 20,000/- and her younger daughter is studying 5th class. Their group got the best group award, and their group was sanctioned Rs. 1 lakh from the government as loan.

Now her livelihood has totally changed and the family members are living happily. Before joining SHG group she used to work hard for getting food to all her family members. Now she saves money Rs. 50/- per month.

Smt. Nagamma, Nimmaluru

Cast Study-13

Manorama is 37 years old woman separated from her husband and belongs to backward community. She got married at the age of 18 years. Her marriage was arranged by her parents. Her husband was an alcoholic. She has one son and one daughter. Son is doing carpentry work. Her daughter is 15 years old and studying 10th standard and her son studied up to 6th standard. She is working in private school as a sweeper. She gets Rs. 400/- per month. She is a literate women. She joined SHG group in the year 2000 and the group is Rohini.

She spends her leisure time in making leaf plates. She got a loan amount of Rs. 1000/- for making leaf plates. All the family needs are to be met by her earnings alone. She is not having any debts. She sells the leaf plates to improve the financial position. She feels that SHG is helping her to meet the demands of her family.

Smt. Manorama, Kuppam Baduru

Case Study-14

Lakshmi Devi is 47 years old. She got married with Venkataramaiah at the age of 15 years. She has four sons. They didn't have education. All of them got married and are living separately. Her husband was doing business. He died by snake bite. After the death of her husband, it is very difficult for her to maintain the family. She saves money Rs. 30/- per month.

After the death of her husband, relatives suggested her to join in the SHG group. After joining in SHG she has given good education to her children. After marriage they have neglected their mother. Both the sons are separated. Lakshmi Devi joined in SHG group in the year 1996. She got subsidy loan Rs. 9000/-. Through SHG money she has started tailoring. Her savings in group is Rs. 30- per month. She has own house. Each member in the group got revolving fund of Rs. 1000/-. She utilises that money as her investment to improve her tailoring shop.

Smt. Lakshmi Devi, Lakshmipuram

Case Study-15

Jayamma is 40 years old widow, belongs to scheduled caste community and is a literate. She got married at the age of 17 years. Her marriage was arranged by the parents. She lost her husband 10 years ago. She has two sons. Her first son is 22 years old and is a labourer. Her second son is 18 years old and is a painter. Both of them studied up to 5th standard. The main source of their income is only from leaf plate making. She got a loan of Rs. 1000/- from DWCRA scheme.

She joined in SHG in the year 1998 and the group is Sarojini. She feels that SHG programme is helpful for her only to some extent. She expressed that the loan provided by the government under the scheme is not sufficient to meet her needs. She needs financial help to develop her leaf plate making business and to improve her income levels.

Smt. Jayamma, Peruru

Case Study-16

Meena Kumari got married to Gundogi Rao at the age of 17 years. Her marriage was accepted by her parents, because he belongs to scheduled caste. She is OC and he is SC.

Both of them were living together separately. Her husband was working in a hostel. They are living in a rented house. She has two sons studying 6th and 5th standards.

At the initial stage of married life both of them used to go for daily wage work. After that she is motivated by M.D.O. to join in self help group. In 1996 she joined in SHG. In 1997 they got revolving Rs. 15,000/- for the group. Each member in the group got Rs. 1000/- with that money and some money from her husband she started a petty shop. Thus after joining in SHG she started saving small amounts from their daily earnings with sincerity and dedication and it help to have a good life.

Smt. Meena Kumari, Chinnagottigallu

Case Study-17

Raheena is 48 years old. She got married with Nazir Ahmed at the age of 15 years. She has three daughters and one son. Her husband was a labourer. She was a house wife before joining in SHG. She studied ûpto 3rd class. Her husbands income was not sufficient for their family survival. So, she did not send their children to school. She wanted to become a labourer but her husband did not allow her to go out.

She was motivated by her neighbours, to join in SHG group. She convinced her husband telling that it can help them for the survival of the family. She joined in Lakshmi Saraswati group in the year 1997. In 1998, they received revolving fund Rs. 1000/-. The whole members in the group started super bazaar with revolving fund received and all the members are taking part in maintaining the super bazaar. In 1998 again they got Rs. 10,000/- and Rs. 9000/- as revolving fund. At the beginning she was paying Rs. 30/- per month as savings. Their group was sanctioned Rs. 1 lakh from the government as loan.

Now, she says that SHG has brought about a change in their lives and now they are living happily with both the incomes of her and her husbands. She is saving Rs. 50/- per month. She even deposited some amount is fixed for her elder daughter's marriage. Now, she is confident to perform her daughter's marriage.

Smt. Raheena, Malagamudi

Case Study-18

"Mummy our vehicle is coming"

My name is Penchalamma. I belong to Tukivakam village of Renigunta mandal in Chittoor district of Andhra Pradesh.

SHG programme saved my life. My children and myself are very much thankful to the programme.

Our Colony

I am residing in the Harijan colony. Government have provided us with quarters. All the women of the Harijan colony are engaged in stone crushing. It is a very hard job but we have to do it to earn our livelihood.

My Health

I gave birth to five children and also three more abortions. At the time of third abortion, I adopted some country methods. I was joined in the hospital for treatment. I was there for one month.

Warning from Doctors

Doctors warned me and my husband also that any more pregnancy will lead to my death. I become anaemic. I was not even able sit and do my household work. Very often I am getting fever.

My Wish

I want to get myself operated after the birth of my second child but my husband refused for that.

My Husband Loves Me but--------

My husband loves me but he never gave his consent for family planning operation. He never heard the advise of local doctors and nurses. Sometimes he did not allow them to step into my house. He used to ask them many questions.

1. "Who will look after my children if anything happened to my wife after getting operated"?
2. "When she is in bed. I can't mange the family with my earnings. Who will support us"?
3. "Who will look after my children when she is in hospital"?
4. "God has given why should be object"?

My Mother

I requested my mother to convince my husband. But she also supported my husband. She told me "I gave birth to 12 children. I am healthy. Who do you worry so much".

Mental Agony

THE THOUGHT OF ONE MORE PREGNANCY FRIGHTENED ME A LOT. I WON'T GET SLEEP DURING NIGHTS. LYING BESIDES MY INNOCENT CHILDREN WHO ARE SLEEPING I WEPT SO MANY NIGHTS.

Who will look after them if anything happened to me? Who will convince my husband and save me from this haveoc?

SHGs

All the Harijan women were organised into three self help groups. We got Rs. 1,000/- each and we spend that amount for transportation of stones from far away places. My mother is also a member of SHG.

Thrift and Credit Groups

Sixty Harijan women were organised into three thrift and credit groups. My mother and myself have joined in "Bharathi Thrift Group".

Loan for my Husband

I took Rs. 1000/- loan from the Thrift group. We invested that money in fruit vending and got more profits. My husband expressed his satisfaction.

Narayana my Guru

Literacy classes were started to SHG women. All the women are attending the classes. Because I am sick, I am unable to attend the classes. But I am very much interested. An intermediate student Narayana (18) every day come to my house and made me literate within 6 months. Though he is younger to me he is my guru.

Medical Camp

A medical camp was conducted to SHG families in Harijanawada. Free medicines were distributed. My husband and myself alongwith my children were checked up. Doctor pointed out the seriousness of my ill health.

All Attack

SHG officers along with other women group came to my house. My husband was a little bit afraid. He tried to go out. But they stopped him.

An Appeal to my Husband

The entire group requested him to undergo vasactomy. He refused. The group requested him at least allow me to undergo operation. My husband again expressed all his doubts and refuse.

Full Support From the Group

1. We will look after your wife while she is in the hospital.
2. We will sanction the amount Rs. 1,000/- more from the thrift group. You can manage with the money until she can do work.

3. My mother who was already motivated by the group told my husband that she will look after my grand children.

Silence

After hearing all these promises my husband kept silence. Internally he developed some respect towards the programme.

Threaten

Finally the group threatened my husband.

1. If anything happened to your wife we will arrest you by police.

2. You are not eligible for any help from the government.

3. Your wife will be removed from SHG and thrift groups.

Acceptance

At last my husband gave his acceptance just by nocking his head for a while.

Next Day

The group members took me to the hospital on the next day itself. I had undergone family planning operation. All the members and also officers are by my side all the time. But my husband did not come to the hospital.

Welcome

When I was discharged from the hospital and went home my husband welcomed me with a smile.

My children, when
ever they happen to
see the DWCRA/SHG
vehicle they will
dance and shout
Mummy
Our Vehicle is coming.

Smt. Penchalamma, Tukivakam.

Case Study-19

Sarojamma is 28 years old women who belongs to BC community. She is an illiterate. She got married when she was 15 years. Her husband is a cook. He cooks at marriages and functions. When he does not find work he keeps idle. She is having only one daughter who is studying in school.

She was motivated by her neighbours and friends to join in self help group. She joined in Kanka Durga Podupu Sangam in 1995. Now she is the second leader of the group. She saved Rs. 30/- per month when she joined the group and now she is saving Rs. 50/- per month. Her group consists of 13 members.

She started bangle business with the matching grant of Rs. 1000/- received from the government. She moves around villages and sells bangles. Her husband's work is being seasonal, they suffered for money before she joined in the group, after that a gradual change has come in their lives. She cleared all the debts and petty hand loans. She took loan from her sangam for reconstruction of her thatched hut. Now cleared that loan also. She is not at all received any help from her husband. Being motivated by her friends and neighbours she could able to raise her status of living. She received gas connection, recently under Deepam scheme. She is thinking of opening a small bangle shop in her village.

Smt. Sarojamma, Cherlopalli

Case Study-20

Radhamma is 35 years old. She got married at the age of 29 years. Her's is an arranged marriage by her parents. She got two daughters and one son, now they are all going to schools. Her husband has a bullock-cart and he transports goods/materials over it.

She spent all her time as an ordinary house wife before she joined in self help group. After joining in self help group she took up tailoring activity. She has undergone one year training at Mahila Pranganam, Tirupati. She purchased sewing machine with the loan amount taken from group savings.

Her group name is Rajyalakshmi Podupu Sangum. It started with 10 members in 1997 with a monthly savings of Rs. 300/-. Now 15 members are there in the group and she is the group leader. The savings amount also rose to Rs. 50/- per month per head. They also lend loans to their group members with 2 per cent rate of interest. Recently they received matchin grant of Rs. 15,000/- and also 'gas connections' to six senior members in the group.

She says that self help group scheme helped her a lot to earn some supporting income to her family. The demand for her work is also good. She constructed a small house also with her savings. *Smt. Radhamma, Tirupati.*

Case Study-21

Padmalatha SHG group is located in Chittoor district of Tirupati Rural mandal. On the whole 40 groups are functioning in Chittoor. Among the 40 groups Padmalatha group is one of the oldest group in this location. It was started in 1995 with 10 members. Among the members three of them are Brahmins and the rest belong to Kapu community. The founder member of the group, Ms. Vijaya Lakshmi, is the president of this group. Under her dynamic leadership this group became a successful group. Being the pioneer of her own group she was responsible for motivating and forming the other 40 groups. They are also under her supervision today. Though Ms. Vijaya Lakshmi was studied only up to 5th class, the Village Development Officer motivated her to take up training to enable her to start self employment and improve her economic status. First she underwent six months training in tailoring, which helped her not only to improve the economic status but also to get self-confidence. It also motivated her to form self help group. Meantime her interest in continuing education made her to appear for 7th class through open university.

Compelled by the economic conditions of the family coupled with her hard work and enterprising qualities she started food producing and Agarbathi making units through her groups. Though she comes from a traditional Brahmin family she has respect for dignity of labour and according to her, she does not fear any one as long as she is doing the right things. Even her family members, especially her brother was against her moving around and selling food products. He even offered her for a monthly payment of Rs. 1500/- but she declined this offer. She said that for a few months they would give and then they might stop. Instead of depending on her brother and others she adopted her own safe approach. She was quite firm and confident in her activities. However she received full co-operation from her husband, who is a priest in small temple. In addition, her good communicative skills, good manners and behaviour and leadership qualities made her a good leader and a very good sales person. Today she is a role model for all other members of the 40 groups in this area. She does not hesitate in fighting for demand for the rights and benefits of the new schemes provided to the SHGs. That shows her self confidence and boldness. She exhibits wonderful organizational abilities while managing the functioning of various groups. She is very modern in her outlook and this quality is demonstrated in various aspects of her life. She has cultivated the habit of reading newspapers to learn about the current affairs and news about the government policies and programmes. She bought a Television under her group mainly to watch news and other useful developmental programmes rather than to watch entertainment activities. She also motivated her group members to become literate through 'Akshara Sankranti' programmes. Besides she motivated all group members to adopt family planning with one or two children. She also motivated and created awarness about the importance of utilization of health services especially during pregnancy and the use of hospital for delivery. She also enlightened the women to avoid child marriage and persuaded parents to send girls for higher education. Her only daughter is now studying at 8th class, she is aspiring to become a collector, after observing the various dynamic activities of the local collector.

For children's future Ms. Vijayalakshmi has taken up LIC policies for her two children. The multi-dimensional activities and personal traits enabled her to take independent decisions leading to autonomy and empowerment. It is fascinating to learn that she is empowered with knowledge on most of the recent programmes of government. All these enabled her to become a successful leader of the SHG.

Smt. Padmalatha, Atturu

Conclusion

The self help groups (SHGs) are informal voluntary association of people formed to attain a collective goal, people who are homogenous with respect to social background, heritage, caste or traditional occupations come together for a common cause to raise and manage resources for the benefit of group members. 'All for all' is the principle behind the concept of self help groups. It is mainly concerned with the poor and it is for the people, by the people and of the people. SHGs, a mini voluntary agency for self help at the micro level has been a focus on the weaker sections particularly women for their social defence. SHGs has got great potential in creating awareness on day-to-day affairs, promoting in savings habit, developing self and community assets, increasing the income level, increasing the social power and development. The concept of SHGs generates self confidence, self security and self reliance. Self help groups broadly go through three stages of evolution :

- Group formation
- Capital formation through revolving fund and skill development.
- Taking up economic activity for income generation.

SHGs is therefore, small economically homogeneous and affinity group of rural poor which voluntarily agrees to contribute to a common fund to be lent to its members as per group decision, which works for group's solidarity, self and group awareness, social and economic development in the way of democratic functioning.

Not withstanding the above challenges, it may be concluded through collective action and social ideology of development. SHGs are fast emerging as "Women's Movement" throughout the nation and especially in Andhra Pradesh where 50 per cent of such SHGs in the country have been formed. The activism with women's movement has influenced policy and planning of the government for development and empowerment.

BIBLIOGRAPHY

BOOKS

1. Abdur R. (1998)—Management of Development in Growth with Equity, Excel Books, New Delhi, 1998.
2. Arun K. Singh. Epowerment of Women in India, Manak Publications Pvt. Ltd., New Delhi, 2000.
3. Bandura Albert. Social Foundation of Thought, Eglewood Cliffs, NJ, Prentice—Hall, 1986.
4. Baxamusa Ramala M and Hema Subramanian, Assistance for Women's Development for National Agencies : Employment Programmes. Popular Prakashan, Mumbai, 1992.
5. Baxamusa Ramala M., and Shobha Joshi. Assistance for Women's Development from National Agencies : Development Programmes. Popular Prakashan, Mumbai, 1992.
6. Bhatt Ela, "Beyond Micro-credit" : 'Structures that increase the economic power of the poor', SEWA Academy, Ahmedabad, 1996.
7. Binita Verma. Exploitation of Women Labour in India—Employment Pattern and Wage Discrimination, Deep and Deep Publications, New Delhi, 1993.
8. Boserup Ester. Women's Role in Economic Development. St. Martin's Press, New York, 1970.
9. Carr Marilyn et al, Speakingout—Women's Economic Empowerment in South Asia, Vistaar Publications, New Delhi, 1997.
10. Chowdary, The Indian Womens Search for Economical Development, Vikas Publishing House (P), Ltd., New Delhi, 2000.
11. Chowdary. The Indian Womens Search for Economical Development, Vikas Publishing House (P), Ltd., New Delhi, 2001.
12. D'Silva. Formation of Self Help Group Federation, Adilabad District, Andhra Pradesh, India, 2001.

13. Devadas, Economical Development of Indian Women, Rathan Publications, New Delhi, 1998.
14. Dhan Foundation, Banking with Self Help Groups, Resource and Research Centre, Madhurai, 1998.
15. Dube S.C. India's Changing Village; Human Factors in Community Development, University Press, New Delhi, 1998.
16. Gain and Satish, Self Help Groups in Rural Development, Dominant Publications and Distributors, New Delhi, 1996.
17. Griffen Vanessa (ed). Women Development and Empowerment : A Pacific Feminist Perspective, Asian and Pacific Development Centre, Kuala Lumper, 1987.
18. Ghosh, et al (1998). Women and Entrepreneurship in India in Entrepreneurship and Innovation, Models for Development, Sage Publications, New Delhi, 1998.
19. Jyothi Mitra (1997). Women and Society—Equality and Empowerment, Kanishka Publishers, New Delhi, 1997.
20. Khan S.S. (2000). Entrepreneurial Development, S. Chand and Sons, New Delhi, 2000.
21. Karl Marilee., Women and Empowerment Participation and Decision Making : Zed Books Ltd. London and New Jersey, 1995.
22. K.G. Karmakar, Rural Credit and Self Help Groups : Micro Finance Needs and Concepts in India, Sage Publications, New Delhi, 1999.
23. Kurtz L.F., Self Help and Support Groups, A Hand Book for Practitioner, Sage Publications, New Delhi, 1997.
24. Leelamma Devasia and V.V. Devasia, Empowering Women for Sustainable Development, Ashish Publishing House, New Delhi, 1994.
25. Leela Gulati, The Female Poor and Economic Reform in India, A Case Study in Women and Development (ed). Krishna Ahooja—Patel S. Uma Devi & G.A. Tadas, Har Anand Publications, New Delhi, 1999.
26. Leslie J. Calman, Toward Empowerment, Women and Movement Politics in India, Bouldre, West View Press 1992.
27. Margaret Hall C, Women and Empowerment, Hemisphere Publishing Corporation, Washinton, 1992.
28. Mahajan V.S., Women's Contribution to India's Economic and Social Development, Deep and Deep Publications, New Delhi, 1993.

29. Mahajan and Madhurima, Family Violence and Abuse in India, Deep and Deep Publications, New Delhi, 1995.
30. Mitra Jyoti, Women and Society—Equality and Empowerment, Kanishka Publishers, New Delhi, 1997.
31. Murthy. S. Women and Employment, RBSA Publishers, Jaipur, 1999.
32. NABARD, Banking With the Poor, Financing Self Help Groups, NABARD, Hyderabad, 2000.
33. Narasaini Laxmi and Naidu V.G. (1998). Role of Banking in Rural Development, Discovery Publishing House, New Delhi, 1998.
34. Panandiker S. Problems and Prospects of Self-employed Women in Women and Development, Vol. 3, Discovery Publishing House, New Delhi, 1991.
35. Parthasarathy G. Economic Impact of Women's Thrift and Credit Societies, Institute of Development and Planning Studies, Visakhapatnam, 1995.
36. Pillai J.K. Women and Empowerment, Gyan Publishing House, New Delhi, 1995.
37. Ponna Wignarja (1999). Women, Poverty and Resources, Sage Publications, New Delhi, 1999.
38. Puhazhend V. and K.J.S. Satyasai, Micro-Finance and Rural People : An Impact Evaluation, NABARD, Mumbai, 2000.
39. Rajeswari M. and Samangala P. Women Entrepreneurs—A Scan on their Problems and Prospects in Women Entrepreneurship, Issues and Strategies, Kanishka Publishers, New Delhi, 1999.
40. Rutherford Stuar. The Poor and Their Monet, an Essay About Financial Services for Poor People. Institute for Development Policy and Management, University of Manchester, 1999.
41. Sakuntala Narasimhan, Empowering Women, An Alternative Strategy from Rural India. Sage Publications, New Delhi, 1999.
42. Sangeetha Purushothaman, The Empowerment of Women in India, Grassroots Women's Networks and the State, Sage Publications, New Delhi, 1998.
43. Shanthi K. (ed), Empowerment of Women, Anmol Publications Pvt. Ltd., New Delhi, 1998.
44. Dr. B. Suguna, Empowerment of Rural Women through Self Help Groups—A Perspective Published in a book titled

Empowerment of People : Grassroots Strategies and Issues Edt. by R. Venkata Ravi, V. Narayana Reddy and M. Venkataramana, Kanishaka Publishers, New Delhi, 2004.

45. Swarnalatha, E.V Empowerment of Women Through Self Help Groups, Discovery Publishing House, New Delhi, 1997.
46. Trakur H.K., Women and Development Planning, Vikas Publishers House, New Delhi, 1988.
47. Thomas Fisher & M.S. Sri Ram, Beyond Micro-Credit, Putting Development back into Micro-Finance, Vistaar Publications, New Delhi, 2002.
48. Venkata Ravi, Narayana Reddy and Venkata Ramana (Edt), Empowerment of People—Gross root Strategies, Kanishka Publications, New Delhi, 2004.

JOURNALS

1. Archana Sinha, Types of SHGs and Their Work, Social Welfare, Vol. 48, No. 11, February 2002.
2. Agnihothri, Self-Employment and Entrepreneurship Development Programmes, Journal of Social Work, Vol. 13, No. 5, May, 1995.
3. Anuradha Dutta, Empowerment of Women—Some Reflections, The Journal of Women's Studies, Vol. 2, No. 1, April-September, 1997.
4. Archana G. Self Help Groups, Innovations in Financing the Poor, Kurukshetra, November, 2001.
5. Avasthi P.K. et al (2002). Working and Impact of Self Help Groups on Economic Status of Women in Watershed Areas of Madhya Pradesh, Indian Journal of Agricultural Economics, 56(3), June, 2002.
6. Basker R.L. The Politics of Empowerment. Social Work. Vol. 4, No. 2, March, 1991.
7. Bennet L., M. Gold Berg and P. Hunte, "Ownership and Sustainability : Lessons on Group–based Financial Services from South Asia", Journal of International Development, 8(2), 1996.
8. Chandra Shanti Kohli, Women and Empowerment, India Journal of Public Administration, July-September, 1997, Vol. XLIII, No.3.
9. Bhagya Lakshmi J(2000). Women in Development, Employment News, 25(3), 2000.

10. Bharat Dogra (2002). Women Self Help Groups : Kindling Sprit of Enterpreneurship, Kurukshetra, September, 2002.
11. Dr. K. Chaidambaram and Dr. V. Sankarasubramaniam, Factors Influencing Repayment of IRDP Loan-A Study, Kurukshetra, Vol. 47, No. 6, March, 1999.
12. Damayanty Shridharan, Encourage Self Help Groups. Social Welfare, Vol. 44, No.7, October, 1997.
13. Dinakar Rao K. (1992). Women's Savings and Credit Schemes; Three Case Studies, Khadigramodyog, October, 1992.
14. Dogra Bharat. Women Self Help Groups : Kindling Sprit of Entrepreneurship, Kurukshetra, May, 2002.
15. Dr. C. Gangaiah, Progress of Podupulakshmi Groups in Nellore District, Kurukshetra, Vol. 49, No. 2, November, 2000.
16. Ganadhara Rao G. (1995). Dimensions of Rural Non-farm Employment of Women, A case in Andhra Pradesh, Journal of Rural Development, Vol. 14(1), 1995.
17. Gautam N and Sing. Development of Women and Children in Rural Areas. An Appraisal, Kurukshetra, 39(33), 1990.
18. Gopalan Sarala, Women's Development—Paradigm Shift from Welfare of Empowerment, Social Welfare, 43(5) August, 1996, P.32-33.
19. B.K. Gopalakrishna, SHGs and Social Defence, Social Welfare, Vol. 48, No. 11, February, 2002.
20. Gurumurthy T.R., Self Help Groups Empower Rural Women, Kurukshetra, Vol. 48, No. 5, February, 2000.
21. Jayalakshmi K. Empowerment of Women in Panchayats—Experiences of Andhra Pradesh, Journal of Rural Development, Vol. 6, No. 2, April—June, 1997.
22. Jesani Amar "Limits of Empowerment : Women in Rural Health Care", Economic and Political Weekly, May 19, 1990, Pp. 1098-1103.
23. Dr. S.C. Joshi, Micro—Credit not Charity, Social Welfare, Vol. 48, No. 11, February, 2002.
24. Kamata Prasad, Poverty Eradication Strategy, Kurukshetra, Vol. 48, No. 5, February 2000.
25. Dr. K. Kokila, DWCRA Bazaar—Successful Experiment, Social Welfare, Vol. 48, No. 11, February, 2002.
26. Kumaran, K.P. Self Help Groups : An Alternative to Institutional Credit to the Poor. A case study in Andhra Pradesh, Journal of Rural Development, 16(3), 1997.

27. Dr. Lakshmi R. Kulshrestha, Micro Finance : The New Development Paradigam for Poor Rural Women, Kurukshetra, Vol. 49, No. 2, November, 2000.

28. Dr. N. Lalitha, Micro Finance : Rural NGOs and Banks Net Working, Social Welfare, Vol. 45, No. 7, October, 1988.

29. Lalitha, N. Towards Empowerment of Women; Organizational and Managerial Perspectives of Women Co-operatives–Journal of Extension Research Vol. II, No. 1, 1999.

30. Leelamma Devasia & Janey Antony, Social Development Issues in Self Help Groups, Social Welfare, Vol. 50, No. 10, January, 2004.

31. Laxmi R. Kulshrestha. Self Help Groups Innovations in Financing the Poor, Kurukshetra, November, 2001.

32. Laxmi R.K. Self Help Groups Innovations in Financing the Poor, Kurukshetra, November, 2001.

33. Madheswaran S, et al. Empowering Rural Women through Self Help Groups: Lessons from Maharastra Rural Credit Project, Indian Journal of Agricultural Economics, 56(3), 2001.

34. Mohanam S, Micro Credit and Empowerment or Women Role of NGO's, Yojana, February, 2000.

35. Dr. K.R. Murugan & Dr. B. Dharmalingam, Self Help Groups–New Women's Movement in Tamil Nadu, Social Welfare, Vol. 47, No. 5, August, 2000.

36. Dr. K. Murugaiah, Social-Economic Empowerment : Interventions to Enhance Women's Income, Social Welfare, Vol. 49, No. 7, October, 2002.

37. Pal Mariam S, Replicating the Grameen Bank in Burkina Faso. Small Enterprise Development, Vol. 8, No., London, 1997.

38. Patnaik B.K. Gender Justice, Women Empowerment and Maternal Health, Yojana, Vol. 40, No. 11, November, 1996.

39. Puhazhendhi V. and Jayaraman B, "Increasing Women's Participation and Employment Generation among Rural Poor : An Approach through Informal Groups", Indian Journal of Agriculture Economics, Vol. 54(3), July-September, 1999.

40. Raja Reddy R. Self Help Groups–Bank Linkage: A Study in Andhra Pradesh, Journal of Mahila Sadhikaratha, No. 1, Vol. 2, 2004.

41. Raja Reddy R. Self Helf Groups–Bank Linkage : A Study in Andhra Pradesh, Journal of Mahila Sadhikaratha, No. 1, Vol. 3, 2004.

42. Shashi Mittal, Grass roots Finance in Tamil Nadu, Social Welfare, March, 1999.
43. K.R. Sudhaman, Stepping up Growth Imperative, Yojana, Vol. 44, No. 11, November, 2000.
44. Dr. K. Sudha Rani & Dr. D. Uma Devi, SHGs Micro-Credit and Empowerment, Social Welfare, Vol. 48, No. 11, February, 2002.
45. Dr. B. Suguna, Women's Empowerment : Concept and Frame Work, Social Welfare, Vol. 48, No. 9, December 2001.
46. Dr. B. Suguna, Strategies for Empowerment of Rural Women, Social Welfare, Vol. 49, No. 5, August, 2002.
47. Dr. B. Suguna, Empowerment of Rural Women through Self Help Groups (Micro-Credit), ROSHNI, January, 2002.
48. Dr. B. Suguna, An Evaluation of Self Help Groups in Saving and Credit, Journal of Sri Aurobindo Anusilan Society, May, 2003.
49. Sujata Viswanathan, Grouping Women for Economic Empowerment, Yojana, 41(3), March, Pp. 37-42.
50. Sujaya Krishnan, EMPOWERMENT : The Mahila Samakhya Experience, DEEP CALLING, January, 1997.
51. D. Sunder Raj, SHGs and Women's Empowerment, Social Welfare, Vol. 50, No. 10, January, 2004.
52. Dr. K. Surekha Rao & G. Padmaja, Self Help Groups in Tirupati, Andhra Pradesh, Social Welfare, Vol. 45, No. 1, April, 1998.
53. P. Tamil Selvi & Dr. Ratha Krishnan, Role Performance of SHG Leaders, Social Welfare, Vol. 50, No. 10, January, 2004.
54. Dr. D. Vasudeva Rao, Empowerment : Concepts and Clarity, Social Welfare, Vol. 49, No. 9, December, 2002.
55. Zippy Allison, The Politics of Empowerment : Social Work, Vol. 4, No. 2, March, 1995.

REPORTS

1. Andhra Pradesh Statistical Abstracts, Directorate of Economic and Statistics. Government of Andhra Pradesh, Hyderabad, 1995.
2. Adams D.W. and J.D. Von Pischke, 'Micro-enterprise Credit Programmes : Deja vu' World Development, 1992.
3. BASIX, Case Studies on Select Micro-Finance Institutions in India (study produced for the International Fund for Agriculture Development), BASIX, Hyderabad, 1999.

4. Canara Bank, Financing Self Help Groups, (Booklet) Bangalore, July, 1997.
5. Census of India, 2001.
6. Chief Planning Officer, Hand Book of Statistics, Chittoor district, 1995-98.
7. Deptt. of Women and Child Development, Towards Empowering Women, Government of India, New Delhi, 1995.
8. Five Year Plan Documents, 1952-1997.
9. M-CRIL 2001), M-CRIL Report, Micro-Credit Ratings and Guarantees, International Limited, New Delhi, 2000.
10. MYRADA, The MYRADA Experience : A manual for capacity building of Self Help Groups, MYRADA, Bangalore, 2000.
11. NABARD, SHG-Bank Linkage Programme : Status as on 31st March 1998 NABARD, Mumbai, 1998.
12. Ninth Five Year Plan, Vol. 11, Government of India, New Delhi, 1997-2002.
13. Prasad Hemalatha, Economic Development of Rural Women : Case Studies of IFAD & DWCRA, National Institute of Rural Development (Unpublished Report), Hyderabad, 1996.
14. Shramshakti : Report of the National Commission of Self-Employed Women in the Informal Sector, Department of Women and Child Development, 1998.

PAPERS/UNPUBLISHED PAPERS/MONOGRAPHS

1. CDF (Cooperative Development Foundation), (1993), "Women's Thrift Co-operatives and External Funding", Unpublished Paper (August), CDF, Hyderabad.
2. Prathama Bank (2000), SHGs and Prathama Bank, Unpublished Mimeo, Moradabad, India.
3. NABARD (1998), "Status Paper on Self Help Groups Bank Linkage Programme as on 31.03.1998", Micro Credit Innovations Department, NABARD, Mumbai.
4. Shylendra H.A., (1999), Micro-Finance and Self Help Groups (SHGs) : A study of the experience of two leading NGOs, SEWA and AKRSP in Gujrat (India), Research Paper 16, Institute of Rural Management, Anand.

NEWS PAPERS

1. The Hindu, Dec 18, 1993.
2. Employment News, 30 August-5 September 1997.

3. The Hindu, Interface, December 27, 1998.
4. The Hindu, Interface, January 3, 1999.
5. The Hindu, Interface, February 21, 1999.
6. Enadu, Daily News Paper, March 1, 1999.
7. The Hindu, Interface, March 28, 1999.
8. The Hindu, Interface, April 11, 1999.
9. The Hindu, Interface, April 25, 1999.
10. The Hindu, Interface, May 2, 1999.
11. The Hindu, Interface, May 23, 1999.
12. The Hindu, Interface, June 20, 1999.
13. Enadu, Daily News Paper, November 9, 1999.
14. Enadu, Daily News Paper, November 10, 1999.
15. The Hindu, Interface, November 14, 1999.
16. The Hindu, Interface, December 9, 1999.
17. The Times of India, December 29, 1999.
18. Enadu, Daily News Paper, April 20, 2000.
19. The Hindu, Interface, May 5, 2000.
20. The Hindu, Interface, July 15, 2000.
21. The Hindu, Interface, July 23, 2000.
22. The Hindu, Interface, July 31, 2000.
23. The Hindu, Interface, September 5, 2000.
24. The Hindu, Interface, September 11, 2000.
25. Enadu, Daily News Paper, October 2, 2000.
26. The Hindu, Interface, October 13, 2000.
27. The Hindu, Interface, November 6, 2000.
28. The Hindu, Interface, December 18, 2000.
29. The Hindu, Interface, February 25, 2001.
30. The Hindu, Interface, February 28, 2001.
31. The Hindu, Interface, April 12, 2001.
32. The Hindu, Interface, June 12, 2001.
33. The Hindu, Interface, June 25, 2001.
34. Enadu, Daily News Paper, December 29, 2001.
35. The Hindu, Interface, January 6, 2002.
36. Enadu, Daily News Paper, January 8, 2002.
37. Visalandhra, Daily Newspaper, March 31, 2002.

Index

S

T

U

V

W